Desert Sage Memories

Edited by Judy Osgood, Sunriver, Oregon
Published by RSVP, Bend, Oregon

Illustrated by: J. Anson, D. Mahoney, M. McAuliffe, M. Miller and J. O'Brien
Cover Watercolor: John O'Brien, Bend, Oregon
Book Design and Layout by: Terry McShane, Chris Miao and Linda West
Photo Credits: Submissions by story authors and Joyce Gribskov
Story Material: Story tellers, COCC Oral History Class taped in 1977
by Gretchen Williver and Redmond Historical Commission

The contents of this book are a collection of memories of long-time Central Oregon residents. These oral histories were recorded by volunteers. The objective is to foster a sense of community and connection through first-hand accounts of local history. RSVP does not assume liability for the accuracy of this information.

ISBN: 0-9704990-1-9
Published and printed in the United States of America
First Printing, 2002

Acknowledgments

RSVP would like to thank the following volunteers for their invaluable assistance:

Executive: *Terry McShane, Judy Osgood and Helen Rastovich*

Editor: *Judy Osgood*

Interviewers & Writers: *Charlene Blahnik, Dave Blahnik, Barbara Baumgardner, Joanne Byrd, Lorna Cerenzia, Rita Dutton, Shinann Earnshaw, Don Ellis, Beth Evans, Karen Goodman, Dick Gorman, Joyce Gribskov, Carol Illinik, Harriet Langmas, Cynthia Larkin, Rosa Lewis, David Lowe, Jim McGrath, Raymond Miao, Jay Moberly, Shelley Palmer, Leo Rosengarth, Vincent Rosengarth, Judy Osgood, Helen Rastovich, Julie Ross, Jerry Shepard, Brooke Snavely, Sharon and Larry Snell, Martha Stranahan, Phyllis Stuewig, Carol Swift, Pauline Teron, Clara Varcoe-Lasher, Gretchen Williver, and Laura Wonser*

Typing and Transcribing: *Beth Evans and Chuck Grossman*

Art: *Joyce Anson, Denise Mahoney, Mary McAuliffe, Mary Romano Miller and John O'Brien*

Layout: *Kari Haller and Terry McShane*

Historical Resource: *Helen Rastovich, Dan Rastovich and Jane Schroeder*

Sales/Marketing: *Dick Gorman, Elsa Gulko, Jim McGrath, Lynn Murphy, Marcella Radke, Helen Rastovich and Jane Schroeder*

Assistance: *Beth Evans, Jane Fitzgerald, Kari Haller, Ray Miao, Lynn Murphy and Norma Ploen*

Proof Readers: *Shinann Earnshaw, Pat Minney and Lynn Murphy*

Pinch Hitters: *Chuck Grossman and Kari Haller*

Girl Wonder: *Judy Osgood*

Boy Wonder: *Ray Miao*

Special thanks to those who shared their stories. All of the information gathered served as a valuable resource.

Having read these stories, I feel as though I have met these people and I know them. They have given me roots in these changing times...

These stories are first-hand memories distilled over time. They are presented as they were told.

Proceeds from the sale of this book are used to sustain RSVP programs.

Retired and Senior Volunteer Program
St. Charles Medical Center
2500 NE Neff Road
Bend, OR 97701

Tele: 541 388-7746

Foreword

There is something about this Central Oregon country that attracts strong people and brings out the best in them.

• People like Reub Long, whose insatiable curiosity provided the understanding he needed to live in harmony with the rhythms of the desert and succeed where most others failed.

• People like Fanny Regnier, whose resilient nature kept her going when the government took her land for an air base and told her to move.

• People of great faith and vision like Penny Penhollow whose original Lord's Acre sale and barbecue has endured and inspired generations.

• People like Bev Clarno, whose childhood challenges prepared her for tough fights in the Oregon Legislature.

• And People like Bill Healy and Don Peters, whose steadfastness and determination resulted in the development of Mt. Bachelor.

Their stories are fun, exciting, interesting, amazing and sometimes downright amusing. They are stories of courage and stories that illustrate a marvelous love of life. But mostly, they are stories of the real people who call Central Oregon home, and all of them are worth reading.

Judy Osgood, Editor

Table of Contents

Foreword....Judy Osgood v

The Early Years

Map of Oregon.... 2
Where Did That Name Come From?.... 3
Oh Those Pioneer Women.... Herbert P. Eby 6
Letha Huettl & Ray Harrington.... 9
Reub Long: The Desert Sage....Judy Osgood 10
Birth Certificate #81....Letha Huettl 13
Ruby Sproat.... 15
Weaning Time for Small Cowboys....Jay Moberly 16
Vern Skelton.... 18
Kathleen Lenore Bacon.... 19
I May Have Been Obstinate....Audra Brennan 20
The Case of the Missing Steers....Dean Hollinshead 23
Kem Scorvo.... 25
Eastern Star Grange....Helen Rastovich 26
Roadbuilding, Pancake Batter and No Accounts....Luther Metke 29
The Rancher and The Nurse....Catherine & Priday Holmes 31
Woolly Migrations....Dominique Verges 34
Life Really Was Different Back Then....Sally Kane 36
Under My Mother's Roof....Rita Dutton & Leo Rosengarth 38
From Old Barns to New Barns....Ray Clarno 40
Old-Time Loggers....Leo Bishop 43
George Alvin Cyrus.... 46

Small Town Stories

It Was Just a Little Town....Phyllis & Stan Sturza 48
The Scale of Things & Times Are Changing....Vadabell Brumblay 49
Everett Van Matre & Porter Houk.... 51
Redmond's Justice of the Peace....Donald Ellis 52
Moonshine....Darwin Clark 53
Leave Me or I'll Haunt You....Bernardine Lowery 54
Flying Teeth and Rolling Planes....Don Hinman 56
The Great Spud Cellar Caper....Jerry Shepard 58
Keith & Aileen Ferguson.... 60
Kem Scorvo.... 61
Helen O'Brien & Anna Eskew.... 62
Shepherds of Sheep and Boys....Vincent Rosengarth 63
Gwen Dent.... 65
Ron Hall and Mervin & Lena Sampels.... 66
How A Broken Axle....Roblay McMullin & Eliza Gallois 67
Arthur Sproat.... 70

Places of Interest

The Museum of Wonders....Frances Turner 72
Before the Hollinshead Barn....Laura Wonser 74
The First Sunriver Development Plan....Brooke Snavely 76
Fly Fishing in the 40s....Lloyd and Joanne Evans 78
It Was This Big!....John Veatch II 79

Faith of Our Fathers

St. Francis of Assisi Catholic Church.... 82
Penny Penhollow and The Lord's Acre....Carroll Penhollow 83
The Pulpit Pounding Preacher....Rev. Mize & Roy Mize 86
Century to Century: Fulfilling the Vision....Judy Osgood 88

Women Who Dared

Les Schwab's Paper Stars....Barbara Baumgardner 90
The Reserve Champion's Doll....Lola Owen 92
Kathleen Bacon.... 93
Born to Ride....Barbara Meyers 94
Rural Photojournalist....Martha Stranahan 96
Destined to Fly....Maggie Sink 98
A Hiker For All Seasons....Myrtice Morrison 100
A Pioneer Spirit Lives On in Redmond....Darleen Dillon 102
Milking Cows, Picking Rocks and Moving Pipe....Bev Clarno 103

Men Who Made a Difference

The Tough Years....Les Schwab 108
Making Your Own Luck....Vern Patrick 110
Respected Editor....Robert Chandler 112

War Years

A Red, White and Blue Job....Loris Farleigh 116
Wartime in Bend....Eva Gassner 118
Central Oregon's Fighting 41st.... 121
Camp Abbot....Diane Roseborough 123
Move! Said the Government....Fannie Regnier 126
Some Fought While Others Were Asked to Farm....Sid Elliott 128
Jack Brinson.... 129
We Danced Away The Years....Jessie Taylor 130

And Then There Was Mt. Bachelor

Bill, the Boss....Kathy DeGree 132
Chris Hart.... 134
Volunteers Build a Mountain....Don & Ollie Peters 135
CAT on the Summit....Ron Robinson, Sr. 138
Skiing Pioneers....Jack & Virginia Meissner 139
The Mitey Mites....Rosanna Duberow 142

The Early Years

I cannot tell how the truth may be;
I say the tale as 'twas said to me.

Scottish Lay

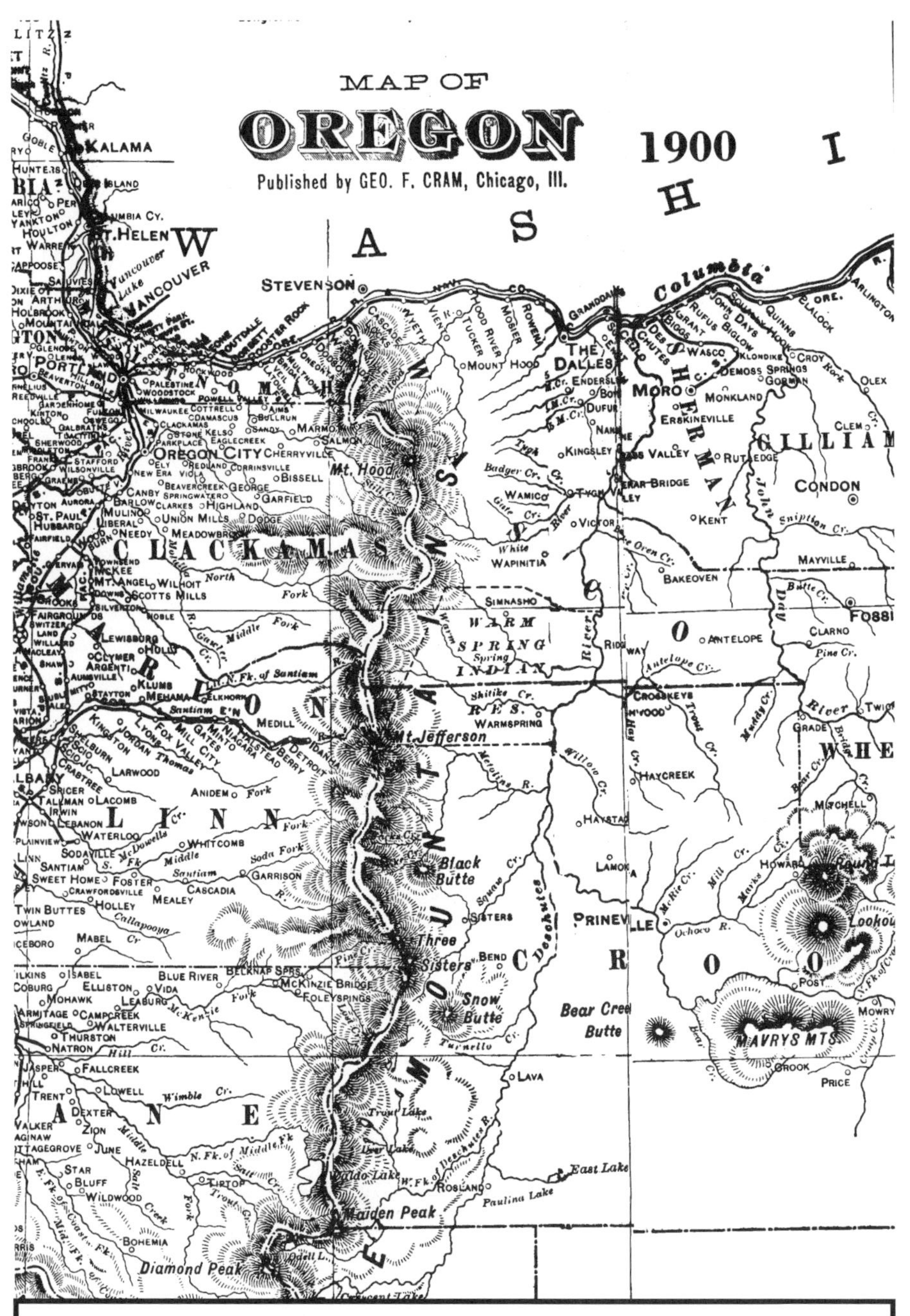

Map courtesy of Jay Vanderford

Map of Oregon, 1900 - Originally published by Geo.F. Cram, Chicago, Ill

Excerpted from ***Treasure Chest of Maps*** *R.N. Preston, 1970*

Where Did That Name Come From?

ARNOLD ICE CAVE - The name came to be applied because of a misreading of a road sign for the Arnold Ranch and an Ice Cave with an arrow pointing in the same direction.

BEND - Originally called Farewell Bend, and received its name because it was at this place that travelers over the pioneer roads had their last view of the river.

BESSIE BUTTE - Named for Bessie Wilkinson, who was the second telephone operator in Bend and homesteaded near the city. It is located 10 miles south of Bend, east of Lava Butte.

BROTHERS - Named after the many homesteading brothers and not a contradistinction to the town of Sisters, northwest of Bend.

CHARCOAL CAVE - Located southwest of Arnold Ice Cave, Charcoal Cave was named by Dr. L. S. Cressman, U of O, because of the large, inexplicable deposit of prehistoric charcoal on its floor.

CULTUS LAKE - Cultus is a Chinook jargon word, quite expressive, meaning bad or wholly worthless, because the area lacks wood, water and grass.

DESCHUTES RIVER - Lewis and Clark discovered the Deschutes River on Tuesday, October 22, 1805, and referred to it by an Indian name Towornehiooks. The Klamath Indians referred to the Deschutes as Kolamkeni Koke. Koke was a general name for stream, while kolam referred to a wild root used for food. The French fur traders called it Riviere des Chutes, meaning River of the Falls of the Columbia.

DORRANCE MEADOW - This meadow is five miles west of La Pine and was named for an early day homesteader, Samuel H. Dorrance. J. L. Melvin killed him later. (See Melvin Butte)

EDISON ICE CAVE - On June 6, 1910, a large fire blazed some 30 miles southwest of Bend. Jack Edison, one of the firefighters, discovered a cool opening in the earth, entered and found an ice cave.

FUZZTAIL BUTTE - Fuzztail Butte is ten miles north of East Lake. A fuzztail was a wild or escaped horse whose unkempt tail was a sure sign of a lack of human attention.

LA PINE - La Pine was named by Alfred A. Aya. The name suggested the abundance of pine trees in the neighborhood. If this form is supposed to indicate a French origin, it is incorrect, as the French word would be Le Pin.

MAIDEN PEAK - Explanations of this name are contradictory. One is to the effect that the mountain, which is at the summit of the Cascade Range, was named in contradistinction to the Three Sisters and Bachelor Butte to the north. Another is that the shape of the mountain resembles a reclining female figure, while a third is that the shape is like a woman's breast. We feel the first one is most likely correct.

MELVIN BUTTE - This butte is in the foothills of the Cascade Range about ten miles southeast of Sisters. It was named for J. L. Melvin, who took up a timber claim nearby about 1902. Melvin got into a controversy with S. H. Dorrance, which is said to have started because Dorrance put sawdust in Melvin's irrigation ditch. As a result of this, Melvin killed Dorrance on the side of the butte. Melvin was cleared by a jury, which considered that he was not to blame for the difficulty.

NEWBERRY CRATER - Nature narrowly missed bringing Oregon two crater lakes almost equal in size and beauty. The crater is located 25 miles south of Bend, and is situated in the summit of the isolated Paulina Mountains and in this crater are two lakes, Paulina Lake and East Lake. The crater was named for Dr. John Strong Newberry, who explored central Oregon for the Pacific Railroad Surveys in 1855.

PILOT BUTTE - Pilot Butte has been a prominent landmark for travelers of many years. Farewell Bend on the Deschutes River was the objective of emigrant trains because it afforded a suitable place to cross the river and was a convenient campground. Pilot Butte was an excellent signal to this stopping place.

PRINGLE FALLS - Pringle Falls on the Deschutes River was named for O. M. Pringle who, in 1902, bought from the government 160 acres of land near the site of the falls, under the Timber and Stone Act. The locality of Pringle Falls is also known as the Fish Trap. Indians guddled salmon at this point, laying on the bank and grasping the fish in the gills as they swam up through the shallow channels.

REDMOND - Redmond was named for Frank T. Redmond, who settled near the present site of the town in 1905. His house was a stopping place for transients. The town was laid out in 1906. The post office was established in 1905.

ROSLAND - The origin of the post office name Rosland is one of the mysteries of central Oregon nomenclature. This office was just a little north of the present location of La Pine, on the old stage road. The name of the office was changed to La Pine on September 21, 1910.

SKELETON CAVE - Skeleton Cave, three miles north of Arnold Ice Cave on the Deschutes Plateau, was named for the accumulation of fossil and modern bones that were found in a natural sink near its mouth.

THREE TRAPPERS - The Three Trappers are three adjoining buttes about six miles east of Craine Prairie Reservoir. They were named in the 1920s to commemorate Toy Wilson, Dewey Morris and Ed Nichols who were murdered in the early spring of 1924 while tending a fox farm at Little Lava Lake. Circumstantial evidence pointed strong suspicion at an escaped convict, who had been seen near Bend, but no direct link was established and the crime remains unsolved today.

TUMALO CREEK - We are not sure of the origin of the word Tumalo, but we believe that it is from the Klamath Indian word temolo, meaning wild plum. This shrub was once quite plentiful in south central Oregon. The Klamaths had another word temolo meaning ground frog, which may have been used to describe the vicinity of Tumalo Creek, but this is conjectural. Some old timers say that the original name was Tumallowa, and meant icy water. Any one of the above explanations might fit the facts, so there you are.

WAMPUS BUTTE - The wampus is a legendary monster of the forest, about which there are many stories. Wampus Butte, named for this creature, is about eight miles west-northwest of La Pine, near the Deschutes River.

WICKIUP - This is an old stockman's name for a point of Deschutes River south of Crane Prairie. The place was a campground for Indians who gathered there to hunt and fish in the fall. They left their wickiup poles standing which gave the place its name.

WIND CAVE - This cave is a mile north of Arnold Ice Cave on the Deschutes Plateau. It is named for the breeze that on warm summer day roars from its 5000-foot tube through the small surface opening.

Excerpted by permission from **Oregon Geographic Names**, *Lewis A. McArthur, Western Imprints, The Press of the Oregon Historical Society, 1982. Copyright 1982 Lewis L. McArthur*

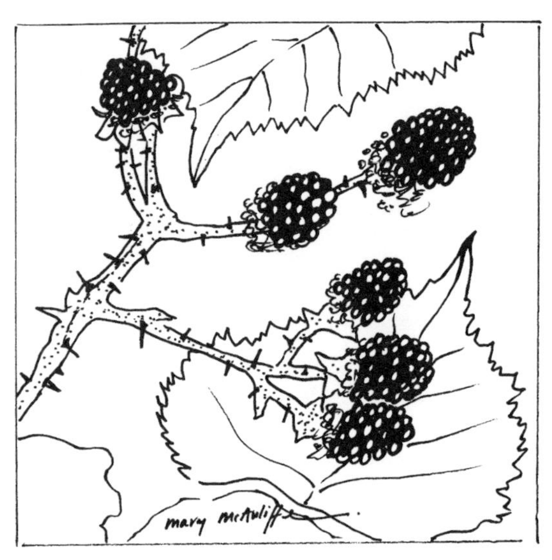

Oh Those Pioneer Women

Herbert P. Eby

Among my mother Lottie C. Eby's papers I found brief notes referring to dates and events beginning with our family's arrival in Oregon in 1905. The picture they paint of those early years, along with a few of my memories, is significant testimony to the strength and fortitude of our pioneer women.

December, 1905 - After loading what few possessions we had on a boat, my mother, Lottie and father, Ezra M. Eby and 9-week old brother, Lewis and I went as far as The Dalles by train. There our belongings were loaded on a covered wagon driven by an old cowboy and we started our overland trek to Central Oregon.

When the baby slept, mother and I walked ahead of the wagon. Nights we stayed with whoever we could find to put us up. One night we spent at a sheep camp on mattresses which were really just large bags filled with straw. All night long mother could hear the mice playing in the straw beneath us.

The next night we fell to bed exhausted in a hotel where the partitions were only six feet high between the rooms. A man and woman could be heard fighting in one of the rooms and a revolver shot was heard, but everyone was too tired to get excited.

Days later we reached our new home, a 12' x 16' barn that Dad had built during the summer out of green boards. By now the cracks had opened and the snow had blown in. It was cold and we had to sleep on the floor because there were no mattresses. Mother hung extra clothes and tablecloths on the walls to keep out the snow, but by morning it was blowing in through the cracks and the roof was leaking.

By the end of the year, less than a month later, mother wrote: "New Years nineteen-six and in our own house with bare board walls with oil paintings (some of them her own and others painted by her mother) the windows with scrim curtains framing a wonderful mountain view (which she always loved) . . . a scarlet and black tablecloth - a wedding present - on the homemade table . . . a cheerful fire in our nice new stove, but minus the crosspiece and one lid from the top, which were lost somewhere on the long trip from The Dalles." By then we were broke. Dad had to get out and earn enough money to keep us going, which meant he sometimes stayed on where he was working.

Dad purchased a range cow for milk. She was very wild and mean and almost killed Mother. That old cow kicked her 'till she was black and blue. On Sunday, when Dad was home, the cow made the mistake of trying to gore him, whereupon, she lost her horns and was quieter.

While Dad was walking to Redmond one night a dense fog came in. Mother grew anxious. She kept listening and about midnight she thought she heard a call from that direction and for two hours she answered that voice to find, at last, that it was an owl. Meanwhile Dad had wisely decided to spend the night in town, as he too was worried he couldn't make it home.

We had brought lots of berry and rose bushes with us from Forest Grove and had set them out long before the irrigation ditch reached our place. Dad had plowed a furrow for almost two miles. He couldn't get it closer to the berry patch and roses than about one hundred feet so mother carried water to them until the canal finally reached. Then, while he worked elsewhere for ten to twelve hours a day, Mother locked the baby and me in the house and tried to keep the water running over the new ground, which had not been property graded. It was tough work but she did what she had to do to carve a new life for her family in the wilderness.

Dad purchased a runt pig, but he couldn't seem to build a pen that would hold it. One day, when the pig got out, someone passing picked it up and took it home with him. Dad borrowed a horse and went after it. The excuse the man gave was that he had none of his own. After they got the pig back Mother wrote in her diary that, "it was lousy and perhaps had worms." To treat it she mixed Lee's Louse Killer in strong soap suds, got into the pen and scrubbed it thoroughly, then gave her a teaspoonful of turpentine in her swill every morning for three days, followed the fourth morning with half a cup of epsom salts. My, how that pig grew after she played veterinarian.

The summer of 1906 was extremely hot and our thermometer reached 112 for several days. Lewis became sick. In search of a cooler location, our family tried camping by the Deschutes River near Lower Bridge, but we went home after two days because Lewis developed bowel trouble. Then his kidneys stopped functioning and he died with convulsions on July 28, 1906. Neighbors made a coffin of pinewood. Mother lined it with white curtain net then sewed a gown for Lewis out of the same material and made him a pillow of pansies. There was no cemetery so Dad offered the east corner of our place, but it wasn't acceptable because it was above the ditch. Instead, land was purchased from Mr. Jaret for the present Redmond cemetery.

Dad had told the doctor that Mother's heart was bad, but when he found her unconscious after the funeral the sawbones wouldn't leave his card game to take care of her. The next day that doctor was run out of town.

Life grew somewhat easier for my mother in the years that followed. But the memories of the old days, the days epitomized by the courage and strength of those pioneer women, will live on in the lives of their children and their grandchildren, and their great grandchildren for as long as their stories are told.

Submitted by Fay (Eby) Drake

Fay M. (Eby) Drake, b.1927 in Bend, Oregon, daughter of Herbert P. Eby. She grew up on a farm on O'Neil Road and then lived as a farm wife in Culver. She served as the deputy clerk of the Culver schools for 25 years.

Letha Harrington Huettl

My mother, Mary Irel Allen Harrington, was born in 1881. Her family lived with Indian families all around them. One summer she stayed with one of those families and learned to speak their language real well. When I was a child we had a natural campground where our big barn was, in Sisters, and everyone camped there on their way through to the valley or the mountains. The Indians came through in the fall for berry picking and hunting. In the evening after dinner, we'd always go out and talk to them. If they'd say something in their jargon so we couldn't understand it, Mom always knew what they said but lots of times she never let on that she knew, not even when my older sister spilled a bucket of berries and one of them said, "My, she's clumsy!"

As told to Clara Varcoe-Lasher

Ray Harrington

Granddad raised horses for the California market. A band of horses ran wild out there and you could run 'em enough to get four or five saddle horses out of the bunch. Then you just had to ride 'em every day till they quit bucking. In the early 20s my dad used the horses on the McKenzie Road when they were building it up through the lava fields. He wrapped the horse's feet in double gunnysacks because the lava was so rough on their feet.

We hauled ice too. Everybody had an icehouse. The horses and wagons would go out on the ice so that they didn't have too far to pack the chunks. By the next morning it would freeze over and it'd be so clear you could see down to the bottom. We'd cut about 2 by 3 foot chunks and load 'em on a wagon. The icehouses were insulated on the outside with sawdust with more sawdust thrown over the ice. That would keep the ice most all summer.

As told to Clara Varcoe-Lasher

Ray Harrington b. 1914 in Sisters and Letha Huettl, b. 1916 in Sisters. Ray worked as a buckaroo in Central Oregon. Leatha cared for others as a nurse at area health care facilities.

Reub Long: The Desert Sage

Judy Osgood

Reub Long described himself as a sagebrush desert rancher, but it was a description that only hinted at the depth of the man. Besides being a rancher who succeeded where others failed, he was a philosopher, writer, historian, naturalist, a student of man, a wit and most of all, a horseman.

He was two in 1900 when his family moved to Christmas Lake where he was raised. His dad had noticed that the people who got ahead were those who owned land, so he bought a meadow watered by springs and moved the family there. Cattle and horses were always a part of their lives and Reub said that by the time he was 12 he and his horse were doing a man's work. When he was seven he bought his first saddle and paid the $13.50 price with money he made himself selling coyote hides and doing little jobs.

Born with an insatiable curiosity, he approached life with a scientist's questioning bent and seemed to absorb everything there was to know about the desert and a whole lot more. "When you live where most everyone else has failed," he said, "you learn to recognize an acorn when you see it. The plants that grow on the desert all have some way of hanging onto water. As a boy grows up there, he must learn to postpone wants, economize on needs and keep his liquid assets from evaporating in the dry desert air. His wants must be few and his needs less."

For most of his life his business was horses. Reub caught wild horses, bought and sold horses and kept horses for people who needed pasture. He supplied bucking horses for rodeos, ran a pack string and raised riding horses. And he had work horses that he hired to contractors for freighting, haying and construction jobs. The one thing he never did with horses was race them. "Horses pretty much dominated the desert," he said, "because they can go thirty miles from water and stay three or four days, even in the summer."

He supplied horses, wagons, horse equipment and know-how in handling horses for two movies: Canyon Passage and Indian Fighter. He was in some of the scenes, as driver of one of the four-horse wagon outfits that tore through stumps, rocks and across rivers when Indians attacked. There may be trick photography in the movies today, but everything they filmed was real and much of it was dangerous. His wife Eleanor, Dean and Lily Hollinshead, Lester Weisenberger and several other friends all worked in Canyon Passage as extras. Reub had so much fun making movies he said he would have done it for nothing.

Reub was, however, a good businessman. "Many big deals were made in land, sheep, horses, cattle, hay and services, with never a word on paper" he said. "In my own case, I soon found the way to get along - drive a hard bargain, then make a liberal settlement. This always left the other man willing to do business again." He made his first deal when he was 16, even owned a pool hall then and made a good profit on it.

Once, briefly, he tried to be a farmer. As he described it he was, "handicapped by some money he had made corraling wild horses" and hired some neighbors to plow and seed three or four hundred acres with rye for him. Normally they consider it a success if the crop didn't die; that year it was rich and thick and four feet high. After he stewed about having to harvest it, his mother asked him why he planted it, and he replied, "I didn't have the slightest idea it would grow."

Although Reub was renowned as a storyteller, there was some question about how much he stretched his stories. "I don't lie to people exactly," he said, "but it's fun to baffle them."

One of the best known comments attributed to him was his statement that, "The reason I've been able to produce some fast horses is that, where I graze them, they have to feed at thirty miles an hour to get enough to eat." He also said that, "If you get to be eighty years old, you don't need to worry because statistics show that a very low percentage of men die after eighty."

Over the years Reub accumulated thousands of acres of desert range where he raised his horses and cattle. To many he is best known for the fact that 9,000 to 10,000-year-old sagebrush sandals were found in a cave on his land. "In modern times Indians were scarce in the desert, but back when glaciers melted and filled the desert with huge, freshwater lakes, this area had more Indians than any other part of Oregon." The sandals, thought to have been left behind by a tribe of which we have no knowledge, were woven out of sagebrush fibers and held on by cords around the ankles. The cave, which is now a national monument, is near Fort Rock. Reub and his wife Eleanor owned a part of that famous tuff ring, which they donated to the state along with some of the surrounding acreage.

Where some speed across the desert and see nothing but sage and sand, Reub spent his life there, learning the lessons the harsh land offered, reveling in its beauty and discovering its secrets.

Once someone asked him if he really lived on the desert. When Reub said yes because his business was there, the stranger replied, "How can you stand it? Don't you ever want to travel?"

"Why, should I travel?" Reub answered. "I'm already here."

*Quotations are taken from **The Oregon Desert** written by E. R. Jackman and R. A. Long.*

Birth Certificate # 81

Letha (Harrington) Huettl

It's true. I was born August 3, 1916 in Sisters, Oregon and my birth certificate is #81. That makes me a real Sisters pioneer woman. In 2001, I was chosen to be the Deschutes County Pioneer Queen. The changes I saw in the 84 years between those two events are nothing short of extraordinary, but it's the memories of the ordinary happenings that mean so much to me.

My brother Ray, who is two years older, was my playmate. When I was three and he was five, our dad started building a new barn. His ladder fascinated us and we wanted to climb it to see how far we could see, but Dad and the hired men always made us get down and out of the way. So one day we waited until they went to the house to eat and then scooted up it when no one would stop us. I can still see my poor mother who came to the back door to call us just as I got straddle of the top. She threw her apron up over her face and started calling Dad to come get us. He and the hired men talked us down because they were afraid we would fall through the rafters.

Around that same time friends came to visit and Cecil, who was my age, went out to play with me. Dad had brought in some wood that had nice charcoal on it so we decided we would be little Negro kids. First we took off our clothes and then we proceeded to blacken ourselves all over. We planned on going in and showing our moms when we got through, but they caught us before we were finished and they didn't like what they saw. First, we got tanned. Then the wash tubs came out in the backyard and the soap and scrub brushes. I was never scrubbed so much in my life and it took quite a while because we were both blonde and we'd made our hair black too. I think it took several washings to erase all the evidence.

There were five or six big bulls in the herds at home. One, we named Wesley; he was so gentle anyone could ride him. Our siblings, Irel and Allen, while on their horses, would lift us up on Wesley and we would ride on his big, fat back. There was another bull that looked a lot like him and sometimes we couldn't tell them apart. One time we were down in the field and mistook this bull for Wesley and we had to climb up in a tree until Allen came on his horse to rescue us.

Despite all those harrowing adventures, I eventually grew up and married Laurence "Lonnie" Huettl in 1934 at our Sisters home. We went together for three years and for the first two he could only see me every other week because gas was so expensive at 35 cents a gallon that he couldn't afford to come more often. We went to ball games in town or just walked. There wasn't even money for a five-cent pack of gum and it was two years before we went to a movie, but no one had any money then so we didn't feel deprived. Our honeymoon was a camping trip to Pringle Falls on the Deschutes River north of La Pine. We moved to the home place on Butler Market Road in Bend so Lonnie could continue to farm. Our lower field is where KGRL Radio station is now.

I probably have more wonderful memories than anyone has a right to and I summed them all up in a biography I wrote saying, "I've had a good life!"

As told to Barbara Baumgardner

Letha Huettl, b. 1916 in Sisters where she attended school. Letha cared for others as a nurse at area health care facilities.

Ruby (Ladrow) Sproat

There used to be lots of rattlesnakes in Sisters. Once my mother killed one on the front porch. The first time I saw a rattlesnake I was out in the fields with my dad. He was irrigating his clover and I was playing in the water in the flume that ran along the fence. When I stepped in this one place I could hear a funny noise. So I was curious and I got out and ducked under there and I said, "Daddy, what kind of a bug is this?" And he said, "Well, what does it look like?" "Well," I told him, "it rattles." He grabbed me by the shirttail and said, "You get away from there. That's a rattlesnake." It must have been cool under that flume or it would have struck.

My granddad made three trips across the country in a covered wagon. He was married about four times. I guess he was hard on his women; they didn't live too long. Then he married my Grandmother, Martha Jane and they had six kids. She was crippled and walked with two canes but she wasn't afraid of the Devil himself.

As told to Clara Varcoe-Lasher

Ruby Cecilia (Ladrow) Sproat was born in 1923 in Baker City, Oregon. She moved to Central Oregon as a young child and has continued to live here most of her life. She was a housewife and worked in a "spud" warehouse for 20 years.

Recipe for Gumdrops

4 tablespoons gelatine
2 cups sugar
3 cups any desired variety fruit juice
1 cup cold water
Vegetable coloring (if desired)
Soak the gelatine in the cold water for five minutes. Stir in the boiling fruit juice, stirring constantly. Turn into tins and let stand overnight. Next morning, cut into squares and roll in granulated sugar. Let stand two days to crystallize.

The Book Of Cookery, *1931, Manning Publishing Co., Chicago, IL, page 14.*

Photo by permission of Raymond Hatton

Weaning Time for Small Cowboys

Jay A. Moberly

Cecil Stearns has been gone from my home for over 36 years. I still feel traces of his presence among my belongings here at the ranch in Terrebonne and at La Pine. He was a little man, probably 5'5" in height, 125 lbs. of weight, stooped by a buckaroo's old age. He spent his last days with me and his brother Gordon, 17 years his junior, both in fragile health, in the Hagedorn home in Prineville.

My credentials were that I had become involved in a cattle-financing arrangement in the Fort Rock area with Gordon, which later included his brother, Carey at La Pine.

At first, I found Cecil hesitant to talk about early days, but after Gordon's death in 1964 he had few people to talk to. Before that time, when the cattle were at La Pine and Fort Rock, Gordon preferred to be at his cabin on the river or at the bunkhouse at the Sink ranch.

Cecil talked about his first time as cowboy and his first time away from home. He was under 12 years of age in 1902. His parents decided he would go with their trusted employee, Jim Black, to La Pine and help deliver supplies to their homestead on the Little Deschutes River. They loaded two horses with pouches tied to their saddles and took off.

As Jim and Cecil rode toward the mountains, he became aware of the vast sweep of country between the canyon in which he was living and the mountains that formed the western skyline. There was no sign of farms or houses; nothing but emptiness. They rode into the clearing in front of the cabin on the Deschutes River just at dark. This was the cabin he had heard about all his life, right on the rushing Deschutes River where the Riverhouse is now located.

This was the cabin where his mother and father came in 1887 on their honeymoon and was spoken of with love and respect. Cecil saw it differently. He saw only an abandoned log shack with a partial dirt floor. A cold wet house. And scary.

His father's trusted friend began ordering him around, making him gather wood for a fire and helping him unload the saddles. Jim gave him a fishing line with bacon on the hook, which he dropped from a log extending from the back porch into the river. Their dinner of bacon, trout and bread was a strange menu for the little boy.

Something began to upset the saddle horses - strange noises, odors and the rain, so Jim brought them inside the small cabin where they were content.

During their meal, Cecil began to panic about his situation. He began to cry and asked that they pack up and ride back to Prineville. Jim flatly refused. He scolded Cecil for being a baby. The conflict mounted. Cecil was ordered to shut up and go to bed. He recalled crying a long time and later waking up in the cold, dark cabin. The only sound was the wind and river, and the horses nibbling at their meal of oats.

In the morning, Cecil renewed his demands to return to Prineville. This resulted in more tears and shouts of anger. Jim eventually reloaded the horses and left. Cecil remembers Jim leaving a slab of bacon hanging from a wire, some oatmeal and a loaf of bread. Jim said he would be back in a couple of days. When he was gone, Cecil really began to panic and went back to bed. When he awoke he managed to get a fire going and got something to eat. He discovered there were two black bears on the back porch and the water log, catching fish.

Cecil could not be sure how long he was alone. He recalled his wood and food supply began to run out. One morning the sun came out, the bears left and Cecil went outside. He heard barnyard noises upstream. He struck out following an old wagon trail. He found the Montgomery homestead. He remembered a warm welcome from Mrs. Montgomery.

Although he was afraid of Jim Black for many years, he realized Jim did the best he could with a crying child, being an old, confirmed bachelor. Jim continued to work for the Stearns' outfit intermittently.

My thanks to Marcy and Gerry Stearns for this bit of history, and to Roger Dierking for his recent advice on homestead matters.

Jay spent 40 years working for the General Land Office, its successor, the Bureau of Land Management, and other Federal agencies including the U.S. Navy during WW II. Jay had several articles in Our Public Lands, an Interior Department magazine. He and his wife, Doris, reside in the Smith Rocks area east of Terrebonne.

Vern Skelton

My parents homesteaded at Odin Falls about four miles north of Cline Falls. Dad had an old pipe and Pedro tobacco. I wanted to smoke that pipe so very bad. One day he handed it to me to keep going for him while he went out to the barn. When he came back in there was a neighbor with him. I began to feel a little sick and the old neighbor started telling stories of boys he had known who had smoked a pipe and gotten so sick they died. You know it wasn't but a short while till I wished I could too!

The winters were cold and long with lots of snow. We did not have any overshoes so when we went out we wrapped gunnysacks around our shoes and legs to keep our feet dry and warm—not so good when it came to a thaw. In 1919 it snowed four feet. I rode a large workhorse to feed cattle. My feet were tucked up behind me but my knees still drug in the snow. It took me an hour to go one half mile.

Excerpts from Homestead Memories
by Vern Skelton, 1964
Submitted by Clara Varcoe-Lasher

Vern Skelton, b. 1898. He farmed the land homesteaded by his family four generations ago.

Kathleen Lenore Bacon

When we were kids, the threshers that were used for harvesting separated the grain from the straw. The grain came down a metal chute into burlap bags, which were taken off when full, sewed shut with string and stacked, while the straw that came out the back end was blown into a stack.

One time my brother Bob and I put burlap sacks over our heads and sat under the straw being blown out. My granddad was driving the team in to unload at the thresher. The mule and horse that were the team pulling the wagon, saw us, bolted and ran off, throwing my granddad off the loaded wagon. My dad saw what was happening and ran to head the team off and stop it, for if they hit an irrigation ditch it would wreck the wagon and could injure the animals. Just as my dad got in front of the team he tripped and fell. The mule put on all four brakes as he liked my dad and would not run over him. My dad used to chew plug tobacco and the mule in the team that day was the one dad always gave a hunk to. I imagine Topsy got an extra big plug of tobacco that day. Believe me, when Daddy got back to the thresher with the team, my brother and I were thoroughly spanked and sent to the house. And we NEVER tried sitting under the straw blower again!

As told to Clara Varcoe-Lasher

Kathleen (Skelton) Bacon, b. 1929 in Redmond, Oregon. She grew up in the Cloverdale area. She was a housewife and bookkeeper but also helped as a farm hand whenever needed. Her grandfather and family homesteaded at Odin Falls.

I May Have Been Obstinate, But I Never Poisoned Anyone!

Audra Brennan

I guess you could say I was obstinate since I didn't come as early as I was expected. In August of 1909, a couple weeks before I was born, my parents took a two-day wagon trip from our home at the head of the Crooked River to Prineville to await my birth. They rented a house for a month - two weeks before and two weeks after. The first night they made it to the ranch of Harry Barnes, who took travelers in day or night. Harry wasn't home and while my mother didn't mind cooking and eating there, she felt funny about sleeping in the house with four youngsters and no one home. So we slept in the hay in the barn, though I'm told my dad worried that Harry would come home with the horses and get him with the pitchfork.

In 1915 we moved to Powell Butte and Dad, who was a carpenter, built a home for us. While he worked on it we lived in 2 tents, one of which had been a small circus tent. We put the bedposts in cans of water to keep the ants out of our beds and we were careful not to have the beds touch the tent wall either. A smaller tent served as a cook house.

As a child I worked as hard as I could and felt like I did just as much work as anybody. My brothers and I would grub sagebrush and pile it up just for the pleasure of having a big bonfire at night. We also built ditches for irrigating. The soil was loose, which meant we had washouts every once in awhile. When we did we had to fan the water out and get it where it would do some good as quickly as possible.

There were five schools in Powell Butte when we were kids and every time I tell someone that they ask, “Why five?” “O.K.,” I say, “how far can you walk to school in all kinds of weather?” We walked 2-1/2 miles to our school through juniper and sage, which probably felt like 10 at the time, but the kids who lived the furthest away rode horseback. There had to be a lot of schools to keep the distance we had to go reasonable. My oldest brother carried a .22 to protect us on the way, and no one thought anything of it. One winter there was an epidemic of rabid coyotes. Wouldn’t you know, on a day when he was home sick one came out of the sagebrush and followed us to school. Fortunately for us that particular coyote was timid, but we still walked backwards to protect ourselves.

Our family raised sheep, and when they were old enough we rounded them up in the juniper and took a couple carloads to Redmond and put them on the train. It was fun because we had a lead sheep that was so good everyone wanted to borrow him. One of us would lead him onto the train and make a circle inside the car, then stand by the door and wait while all those other sheep followed him and walked right in. Then my sister and I would put him in the back seat of the car and drive home while my dad rode to the Portland stockyards with the rest of the flock.

My future husband was someone I had known as a youngster when we lived in Prineville. I always said he was one of the meanest boys on the block because he threw snowballs at me in the wintertime. We weren’t exactly friends, but I knew who he was. He was older than I was and finished high school about the time I started.

I met him again after he returned from WW I and went into ranching. At the time I was working as a bookkeeper at a garage in Prineville and one day he brought his car in to be fixed. Later, I was at a dance in Powell Butte with a fellow we both knew and he came along and told my date, “I’m going to take your girl.” That was the beginning of that, but it wasn’t love at first sight. The next time he came to town to see me I was out with that other guy, but he persisted and I finally started going out with him.

When we got married he didn't own anything but a mortgage and some sheep, and then the Depression came along and wiped us out. We were always ranchers, sheep and beef, and we did some shearing and contract haying for the ranches up above Paulina.

When we went on a contract haying trip, we had to cook for a crew of about 8. I did it on a little cast iron stove where the two sides opened up to be ovens and the top was just big enough for the coffee pot and frying pan. It was quite a trip into Bend for supplies so we made it as seldom as possible. As we had to take everything with us, we'd try to camp by a creek or an old well. Then we dug out a hole in the creek and I kept the 10 gallons of cream there that I churned into butter. Of course, we also kept other things there that needed to be kept cold, except for the meat.

My husband and I also did our own butchering for the crew, sometimes beef and sometimes mutton. I was careful not to let the hay hands know it was mutton or they wouldn't eat it, but they liked it if they thought it was wild. We also did some hunting to feed the crew, so they did get wild meat occasionally. It was illegal, but during the Depression the officers kind of looked the other way. When we butchered we put the meat in great big sacks and buried it in the hay in the daytime and got it out at night. We'd take it out of the sack and let it air out and then bury it again in the morning. That way you could keep meat for a week or 10 days during the hottest summer. It may sound risky, but it worked, and I don't think I ever poisoned anybody.

As told to Lorna Cerenzia

Audra Brennan, b. 1909 in Prineville, Oregon. Audra has lived in the Central Oregon area all her life. She worked as a bookkeeper for Ochoco Lumber for 20 years but found plenty of time to ride horses. She lives in Prineville.

The Case of the Missing Steers and Other Bovine Tales

Dean Hollinshead

My dad came here in 1896 from Independence, Oregon to look the country over. When he said he was a-comin' out here, my mother kinda raised a fuss. She didn't want him to come unless he took her back to Independence to see her mother every year. So he did. For ten years, every October 1, he took her back for a month. It took five days over and seven days to come back fully loaded with enough groceries to last us a year.

At that time the country we moved to was called Rosland. Then a big irrigation company came in and bought all that land so they could put in an irrigation system, and the guy in charge wanted to start a new town. He told the people up in Rosland that if they'd agree to move to start the new town, he'd furnish the money. So they moved everything up there with horses. Hauled all the houses, the hotel, the saloon, the post office and the store. They'd jack those buildings up, put logs under them, put a plank floor on the ground and roll the whole thing along on the logs. Took about seven days to go that one-mile distance, and the new town was named La Pine.

The summer range for the Stearns Ranch in Prineville was around La Pine and it was a big hey-day for us kids when they came each year with all their calves to be branded. My brother Cecil and I would go there and we'd work all day long. We'd get a hot lunch at noon and then somethin' to eat at night. We would go about 10 miles back home and sleep a couple hours, and then back we'd go the next day and start all over again. After they were branded we'd help move them to Crane Prairie and Davis Lake. We were paid a dollar a day sometimes, if we furnished our own horse, and we sure felt like we were big guys.

A fella named Pete Eaton had a little ranch on the other side of La Pine from the Stearns spread. One time he was taking six steers to Bend to be butchered, but they stampeded and he lost all six of 'em. About a week later, four of 'em showed up in his pasture. He didn't want to take a chance of losing them again, so he got ahold of my brother, Chet and asked him to haul 'em in to Bend in a truck. So big-hearted Chet let me go out there to get 'em.

We got all four of them loaded and Pete and me were just standin' there by a big mud hole, gettin' ready to go to Bend when he said, "Wait a minute now. I'm goin' over to the meadow, 'cause those other two steers just mighta come in, and we can get 'em and take them along." I just stood there while he went looking for them one last time, and just happened to glance down at the middle of this big mud hole I was standin' by and saw two great big eyes lookin' right back at me! I jumped back a good many feet when I saw them and screamed at Pete to get back over here quick. He come a runnin' as fast as he could. I pointed and said, "What's that?" At first he didn't know either, and then he saw not two but four eyes.

"Ah, them's my two steers," he said. And those two steers were still alive. They just had their eyes and heads stickin' out of the mud hole. They'd been in there for over a week and hadn't died yet. He told me to go ahead to Bend with the load I had and he'd go back to the ranch and get something to hoist the steers outa there with. And he went out there with everything he had, but he couldn't lift 'em, so he had to shoot em.

Another bovine story involved Klondike Kate who lived in the area for awhile. At one point she told my friend Rod Rosebrook that she'd like to have a cow so she could have some milk. Rod sold her one and she kept it for about a year but never got a drop of milk. When she saw him again she said, "I can't get no milk outa that cow." And Rod said, "Well, you gotta have a bull first before you can get milk." So she said, "Oh, I see. Well that won't be any problem at all." Where upon she went over to the neighbors and traded the cow for a bull!

And that's the end of my bovine tales.

As told to Gretchen Williver
COCC Oral History Tapes 1977

Dean Hollinshead, 1897-1983, was born in Independence, Oregon. He lived in the La Pine area until he married Lily Hoard in 1932 and moved to Bend. They bought the property on Jones Road in 1939 that eventually became Hollinshead Park.

Kem Scorvo

When my mother was a child in the 1920s, walking to the neighbors was one of the things they did for recreation. My grandmother would take my mother and her brother, and they'd walk from Deschutes Junction, straight across the country to Pleasant Ridge, which was probably a three or four mile hike. My grandparents were from Denmark and the purpose of this trip was to visit their Scandinavian neighbors. They would just walk there for the day, and then came home again. Of course you couldn't go until the cows were milked in the morning and you had to be home by the time the cows needed to be milked again at night. Another thing my grandparents did was play a lot of cards. It was a big social thing. They would go to one house or another and play cards. But, of course, that couldn't start until after the cows were milked.

As told to Joyce Gribskov

Kem Scorvo b. 1946 at St. Charles Hospital, Bend. She attended school in Redmond, moved away and returned in 1988. Kem works as an RN in the emergency room at St. Charles Medical Center.

Eastern Star Grange
Helen Rastovich

The Grange is a nationwide fraternal farm organization of people interested in agriculture, their rural community and the family. When the Eastern Star Grange was chartered on June 3, 1912, with twenty-six members signing the charter, the Bend area was still part of Crook County.

Initially Grange meetings were held in the Richardson School building, which was located on the corner of Highway 20E and Hamby Road. During this same period a building was being erected by settlers of the area to be used as a community meeting place and for social gatherings. They named the building Grange Hall, later changing the name to Eastern Star Grange Hall, and deeding the property to the Grange.

Wood stoves heated the building but lighting the hall was quite a problem. Kerosene lamps and candles were used first, then replaced with the gasoline lanterns that provided illumination until 1936 when Pacific Power and Light brought electricity to the area. The original hall only had a small kitchen, but a bigger one and a dining room were built in 1935 with donated lumber and labor. Lack of water was also a problem until a cistern was constructed.

In June of 1920, the Eastern Star Grange and the City of Bend hosted the 47th annual Oregon State Grange Convention. Two hundred delegates and their families registered for the sessions, which were held in the old Bend High School Gymnasium. The convention was a major undertaking and the cooperation of the whole town was needed to make it successful.

The biggest problem was finding housing for the visitors. Since the few hotels in Bend were booked to capacity, everyone in the community was asked to open their homes to one or two Grangers.

It was quite an occasion. The whole city spruced up for the Grangers and every merchant in town decorated their windows with many displaying a sign that said, “Made in Oregon.”

On Tuesday, June lst, the opening sessions were held. That evening all the delegates, their families and local residents (totaling 500) were guests of the Bend Rod and Gun Club at a trout feed held at 7 p.m. on the east bank of the Deschutes River, north of the footbridge.

Local anglers spent two days catching the trout from the various lakes and streams in the county. Cooks prepared the fish, potatoes and coffee for the visitors and served them on novel wooden plates provided by the Shevlin-Hixon Logging Company. Each plate bore the Bend emblem and a greeting from the Shevlin-Hixon Company to the delegates. Menus furnished by Brooks-Scanlon Logging Company were printed on Deschutes white pine boards. Delegates and their friends and families sat at long wooden tables and benches erected by the Forest Service. A large bonfire provided light and the Shevlin-Hixon Logging Company band entertained. The Mayor of Bend gave the welcome. On Thursday afternoon the visitors were taken on a tour of the local mills. Refreshments were provided at the Eastern Star Grange Hall, which was six miles east of Bend. A big concern for the Bend Community Club was whether they would have enough gasoline to transport all the visitors to the hall for refreshments. Again the community spirit prevailed and the gasoline was obtained.

S. J. Lowell of New York, National Grange Master, attended the session and advised the delegation that the National Grange would stand behind Central Oregon in their effort to obtain federal aid for the construction of the irrigation projects.

It was a significant accomplishment for a relatively new subordinate Grange to host the 1920 Oregon State Grange Convention, and total community involvement was the key to its success. Obviously it was a good beginning for them because ninety years later the Eastern Star Grange is still active with monthly meetings and dances being held at the hall.

Helen Rastovich was born in Bend in 1935. She married Dan Rastovich in 1960. They have 2 children. She was Deschutes Co. Treasurer, 1965-1997and is Secretary-Treasurer, Eastern Star Grange.

Prohibition Cocktail

2 cups white grape juice
1 cup orange juice
Juice 1 lime
Crushed ice
1 small bottle of dry ginger ale
Fresh strawberries, cherries, peaches or maraschino cherries

Mix the fruit juices, then shake with crushed ice until thoroughly blended. Add the ginger ale, strain into cocktail glasses and garnish with the fruit, cutting strawberries or cherries into halves, or peaches into slices.

The Book of Cookery, *1931, Manning Publishing Co., Chicago, IL, page 38.*

Photo courtesy of Joyce Gribskov

Roadbuilding, Pancake Batter, and No Account Books

Luther Metke

I was a special road supervisor for Crook County and built the high desert road in 1912. Horses was all we had for power and we used to have ta go all the way to Millican to get water for them. Harry Bailey was the County Commissioner. He looked after the roads, and I used to work with him.

The road at that time wound down through the junipers from here to Burns. The old road used to wind down the hill that was so steep that an old Model T Ford, unless it had a full tank, couldn't make it up the hill because of the old gravity system for the gas. There was many a time, when we used to play ball with 'em down there at Shaniko, we'd get caught on that grade with half a tank and we'd have to lift the old car around and back up in order to get out. When our old Model T radiators went haywire, we'd fix 'em with pancake batter. We didn't pour it in; we put it on the outside. If you put it on the outside of those old honeycomb radiators, it would firm up and stop the leak right now.

So, we had to build a road out there in the desert. Locators grabbed everybody they could and located them on claims. They found claims for people and charged 'em a fee, ya know. Usually around $100. They advertised the claims highly and made them seem better than they were - like they were gonna grow fruit and everything.

I had to build the road from here beyond Glass Butte to the Harney County line. The headquarters was in Prineville. Old Commissioner Bailey would put money in the bank that I'd write checks on. He didn't know when I ran out of money until my checks bounced. I used to job out the work to the homesteaders 'cause they didn't have no means and no work. Until they got to trappin' coyotes, that is. They got a $5 bounty for trappin' them and $5 for the hides. That was their only means of support, so they were glad to get the work helping me with the road.

Harry Bailey gave me $7,800 to build that 84 miles of road. All we did was to clear out a road four rods wide. Just took out the loose rock and the sagebrush. We'd run over the sagebrush with a horse grader and blade. Four head of horses on a grader. It wasn't a very good road. It was soft ground and it killed a lot of horses trying to haul loads over it before the road packed down. But that was the only thing there was to a road in those days.

We never kept any books or records or anything. I'd get a receipt from anybody I paid any money to. I'd just hand the receipts to Harry Bailey, and he wasn't too good at keeping records. Jimmy Overturf was one of the first commissioners after Deschutes County was established in 1916. At the first meeting of Deschutes County, he wondered what became of the $7,800 that was appropriated for that road. The only record was the road.

As told to Gretchen Williver
COCC Oral History tapes 1977

Seeds

It isn't what we have
It isn't what we know
The only thing that matters
Is the "good will" that we sow.

By Luther Metke

Luther Metke born in Buffalo, NY, in 1885, served in the Spanish American War and moved to Bend in 1907. He was a poet and builder of log houses. He received national recognition in 1980 when the biographical documentary film "Luther Metke at 94" was nominated for an Academy Award.

The Rancher and The Nurse

Catherine and Priday Holmes

Catherine's Story - I was born in Portland, Oregon in 1910 and lived there until I entered the University of Oregon in 1928, in the second class of a newly formed five-year nursing course. For me that was a dream come true, as I had wanted to be a nurse since early childhood. Our education began with two years at the U. of O. including some liberal arts and science classes. Then we went on to two years in a hospital with an accredited training school and finished with a year of specialization in a chosen field of interest. I had my hospital training at Multnomah County Hospital in Portland, which is now part of the Oregon Health and Sciences University, then finished with a year of public health.

By the time I finished and was ready to enter the work force it was the midst of the Depression and jobs were scarce. Nurses were put on a registry and called in rotation for work. A job could last an hour, a day, or a month. We were paid $7.50 for a 12-hour shift.

In January of 1934 a classmate, Helenmarr Grison and I applied for two public health jobs in Deschutes County. We drove over in my 1929 Plymouth to apply in person and got the jobs starting the next month. In February we drove back to Bend to start work, and I've got to admit that after having lived my whole life in cities, it felt so remote that it was almost terrifying.

Helenmarr and I found an apartment at 238 Hill Street. It had a small wood heater in the living room and a small wood cookstove, which we kept hot with boxwood from the mill. Our rent was $25 and my salary as the school nurse was $90 a month with a $15 car allowance. We wore the traditional public nurse navy blue dress with white collar and cuffs.

I mostly worked with the Bend school children. In addition, I made home calls to check on absences due to illness. During the summer months there was follow-up work and immunization clinics, which the county nurse and I did with the help of several women in the Deschutes County Health Association.

Another public nurse classmate's mother, Mrs. Holmes lived in Lower Bridge and she invited us for a weekend at their ranch not long after we moved to the area. That weekend we met Dorothy's brother, Priday, who was helping his mother run the ranch. Priday and a buddy started visiting Bend to take us on Saturday night dates. Most often we went to county dances held in the Grange halls. The music was always local folks, like the Bud Russell orchestra. At midnight the Grange ladies would serve homemade sandwiches and pies. Well, dancing must have been good because soon Helenmarr, got married. In 1934, just after Christmas I announced my engagement to Priday Holmes. We were married on March 7, 1936, in Portland and many of our friends and relatives traveled there for the wedding.

Priday's Story - My father was the superintendent foreman for the Black Butte Land and Livestock Company, which was made up of five ranches, headquartered at Lower Bridge. In 1918, the Black Butte Company was dissolved and Dad received our ranch as his share in the company.

There was a deep snow that came in December of 1919. It was dry but hard to get around in because there was so much of it. My sisters and I were at school with the horse and buggy when it started. That night our teacher Mrs. Parrott rode home with us as her house was on our way. We just had one horse on our buggy and there was a steep hill it couldn't make it up, so we all had to get out and push. It turned very cold, below zero, and my mother was frantic because she didn't know if we could get home or not.

My Dad was caught in the same storm, trying to deliver cattle he had sold. He herded them through Grandview but could not get them across

Squaw Creek because of high water, so he went back to Squaw Flat for help. With the assistance of three other men he finally got the cattle across the creek, then spent the night at Squaw Flat. All that night the snow continued and the temperature fell to 36 below zero. The next day he left the cattle there and rode his big, stout horse home.

I went to high school in Redmond. After I graduated in 1929 I helped my mother run the ranch and it was to that big house that I took my bride, Catherine.

Fortunately we never had a winter with a snow like that in the winter of 1919, but ranch life in that big house was still an adjustment for my wife as it had no electricity, no running water, and no central heating. Although we had carbide lights, the system rarely worked so we used kerosene lamps and a hand pump cistern from a sink, or carried pails of water from the water ditch at the water supply. There were four wood-burning heating stoves and a huge kitchen range complete with water warming reservoir on the side. On the cool side of the kitchen was a 12 x 14-foot pantry with one-foot thick walls filled with sawdust for insulation. Foodstuffs were stored from floor to ceiling. Laundry was done with a Maytag gas-operated washing machine that had to be run on the open back porch because of the fumes. On the plus side, we did have the only bathtub in Lower Bridge.

Catherine and I raised our family on the ranch and stayed in that big house until we moved to Redmond in 1963.

As told to Don Ellis
Courtesy of the Redmond Historical Commission

Love doesn't make the world go 'round.
Love is what makes the ride worthwhile.

Franklin P. Jones

Woolly Migrations

Dominique Verges

Around 1915 the desert was drying up, and it was at that point that a lot of ranchers began moving their sheep to the mountains where there was lots of good feed for them. They would spend the winter around the ranches in Maupin and Shaniko and then be herded to the Cascades in the spring. Sometimes their migration route went through Bend and across the river up at Tumalo. Sometimes they arrived on foot; sometimes by train.

Near the 3rd Street underpass there were a lot of sheep stockyards. Ranchers would bring their flocks to Bend by train, unload, and keep them in the stockyards for a couple of days before herding them across the sheep bridge near where the Riverhouse is now, and on up to the mountains.

Sometimes they were herded along county roads. When that happened all those little feet really compacted the surface, making the roads almost as smooth as pavement. They had designated routes they were supposed to stay on, but they were always getting lost, and making five or six mile detours. Of course, sometimes they did it on purpose in search of better forage.

We lived on Parrell Road, which was the main highway at that time, and the sheep were often herded right up it. When that happened all of us kids had to guard our gardens and flowers, because they could get through any fence. You could look up the street and you'd see ladies waving their aprons to keep the sheep out of their yards. They would also get hoses and squirt down the sheep and the ranchers as well. And, of course, you could hear the sheep baa'ing as they came down the street.

Before the sheep were herded to the mountains in the spring they were sheared and dipped. In 1923 we had hoof and mouth disease in this area. All the cars had to drive through a trough of dip out there on the highway. People also had to get out of the cars and walk through the damp part near the trough. When I was going to school I was driving 13 miles into Bend and I had to go through the dip trough twice a day. It was a bit of a nuisance, but it got rid of the disease. The main reason the sheep were dipped is that it killed the fleas and ticks.

In the mountains the sheep would be tended by a sheepherder and 10 or 12 good sheep dogs. Running and barking, they deftly controlled their woolly charges, moving them from one territory to another.

Back in the 1930s a lot of sheep men went broke. They routinely borrowed money to feed their flocks during the winter. If the bank wouldn't give them any more money - which happened many times - the bank got the sheep. I remember one bank in Burns foreclosed on a band and the owner drove them right through town and right down Main Street to the bank. Can't you just see that happening today with a herd of sheep making their own deposits in the lobby of one of our fancy downtown banks! What a woolly spectacle that would be.

As told to Gretchen Williver
COCC Oral History Tapes 1977.

Mirror Pond with Pilot Butte Inn in the background on left

Life Really Was Different Back Then

Sally Schilling Kane

My parents were married in 1917 and my dad had an auto parts and tire recapping business. It was nothing like businesses today, but it was quite successful. He was like a doctor always on call, 24-hours a day, 7-days a week. In the middle of the night the phone would ring and it would be someone in Burns or La Grande or some other area, saying they were broken down and needed a part for their car. Dad didn't wait until morning to help them. He would go down to the shop immediately, get the required part, and leave on his mission to rescue the stranded motorist.

That was only one way in which life was so different back then, than it is now. It was a good time to be a kid and for the most part our parents were pretty relaxed about the things we did for fun. Somehow, I think it made us more responsible for ourselves. That doesn't mean they didn't ever worry about us though, or that we didn't hear about it when we stepped over the line.

We loved to go on long hikes, and sometimes Phil Brogan was our leader. One time he got us really lost, and we were out there high in the hills, for a long time. When I finally got home, I got a real bawling out because I was so late. For some reason I had to eat cantaloupe for dinner that night and, probably because of that association, I have never liked it since.

Water played a big role in our lives in more ways than one. We were real waterdogs and lived in our bathing suits all summer. One time we decided to swim across the river from the Brook park to the front of the Pine Tavern. There was a strong current at that time and about three-quarters of the way across I got very tired and was really glad to finally reach the other side. I didn't need a scolding to tell me that was a bad idea: I decided on my own that I'd never do that again.

Then as now, the river was a focal point for social events in the city. The big celebration then was the Bend Water Pageant. I loved to see the water floats go down the river and was thrilled the year my dad's auto parts company entered one and I was the only one who rode on it. That must have been during my last years of grade school because I had long curls. Some of the floats were really memorable. One that made quite an impression on me looked like half a watermelon. All the kids were dressed up in black faces to look like seeds and they tap danced all the way down the river.

Today I'm sure that float would be considered politically incorrect, parents would be afraid to let their kids do some of the things we did, and there probably aren't any "car doctors" anywhere that work a 24/7 schedule. All of which just underscores the fact that life really was different back then.

As told to Joyce Gribskov

Sally Schilling Kane was born in Bend in 1928. She graduated from the University of Oregon and remains a Duck. She had a career in radio and advertising. She returned to live in Bend in 1996.

Under My Mother's Roof

Rita Rosengarth Dutton and Leo Rosengarth

When our mother, Gertrude Sachtjen, arrived from Germany in 1923 the homeland she left was still devastated from the First World War. She was 16 and unprepared for the bleak homesteading life that awaited her in the desert. Although her sister was with her, their parents had not told Gertrude that a marriage had been arranged for Teresa, whose intended husband, John Stenkamp was waiting for them in Brothers, Oregon. Nor did she know what that little settlement, that had been named for the numerous brothers that lived there, including the Tekampe and Stenkamp siblings, was really like.

Mom was of the belief that in America "the streets were paved with gold, and you could have anything just for the asking." Instead she found only a dusty road in front of the single building in town, which was a small clapboard store. The shack she and Teresa moved into was freezing cold. It only had eising-glass for windows, and one small pot bellied stove to get their front and back sides warmed. Gertrude heard the coyotes howling and was so scared, she "just knew they were coming to haul her off." Nevertheless, she lived in the desert for several years before moving to Bend where she eventually met and married Anthony Rosengarth, whose family had also emigrated from Breman, Germany. Dad's father, Anton had heard that you could get land just for the taking in Central Oregon, so he applied for some of that free soil. When Anton and his sons, Anthony and Carl arrived in Bend on Thanksgiving Day in 1912, all they saw was sagebrush, rocks, sand and rabbits, and they asked, "Lord, oh Lord, what have we gotten into?" They had no home and no shelter and it was colder than the proverbial well digger's butt in Idaho. A neighbor, feeling sorry for them, loaned them a tent which they lived in it all winter, while they survived on a monotonous diet of jackrabbits.

Their property was along the road where mother was living with and working for another sister, Hubertina, who had married John Stenkamp's brother, Henry. The most difficult thing for her was to overcome her shyness, which was related to her faltering English. When she arrived in Oregon she didn't speak the language at all, so she tried to teach herself by studying the Bulletin and listening to the few gramophone records the Stenkamps owned.

After she met Anthony, he tried to help her with the language, and as he did so a romance developed and they were married in 1929. His lessons were to prove very important in the future for during World War II, in Bend as elsewhere, speaking German was suddenly taboo.

At that time the area had largely been settled by the Germans who came to farm and the Scandinavians who came to cut timber. When Hitler invaded the Scandinavian countries, it was the beginning of a lot of heartaches for the city's German residents. Suddenly their friendships with Scandinavian neighbors came to an end, and Bend became like two split camps. It was an aspect of the war that lingered after the guns were silenced and the peace treaties signed; lingered until the healing began at home too.

Rita (Rosengarth) Dutton, b. 1931 and Leo Rosengarth, b. 1934 were both born in Bend. Rita worked as a grocery clerk and Leo had a career as a business executive. Both are now nomads and love to travel.

From Old Barns to New Barns

Ray Clarno

My grandfather had a barn in Redmond. It was on what used to be Northwest Market Way, the road past the high school. About a mile down the way. Adams, on my mother's side homesteaded down there. And he raised cattle there around 1912. He built that barn out of rough lumber. It was all pole construction. You always built the barn first, you know. And the house came later. They lived in the barn for a while. Milked on one side and lived on the other side. It was a whale of a barn. Those poles were about 36 feet long. And my Aunt Ruth grew up on that farm and taught school in Antelope. She turns 93 this year.

You know, at that time everyone lived on ranches or farms basically. Like was typical with my grandparents, they had the big barn. Started with a large barn. Horses on one side, milk cows on the other side. In the middle of course was all the hay barn. Then they had the granary at one end. Then they had the old rock cistern up there by the road. Then they had a milk parlor for the milk buckets. Then they had a bunkhouse for hired help. Then they had another building for a chicken house. Then they had another building for a garage and another building for the woodshed. And then they had the outhouse. The outhouse was kind of interesting. This was a real uptown outhouse because it was a two or maybe three holer you know. But they put in a bathroom in the house. So you had the kitchen and this area off of it. And they had the bathroom with a tub and a toilet and a sink. You know, as many years as that was in there, they never used it. They still would go outside to the outhouse. I guess someone said they should have an indoor facility. So they put it in, but they never used it. I know, when it was in, I never used it. We'd still always go to the outhouse. They had two holes; you wonder if several folks ever used them at the same time.

Anyway, the house they built had a root cellar in it. Everybody had a root cellar. You canned venison and beef. And all your fruits and vegetables went in the cellar. It was usually made of this lava rock around here and sort of mudded in. It was separate from the house. Some were dug into the ground and some were maybe half in the ground. Theirs was underneath the house and you could get to it only around the side of the house. You'd open up the doors just like the tornado cellars in the Midwest. In addition, they had the old spuds cellar too. That was the furthest thing from the house. It was clear out in the southwest corner of the ranch. It was scooped out and then kind of built over the top again with rocks and mud. So you'd drive your machinery down at an angle into it. The potato sorter or the tractor would drive down through the center. And that's where you worked. On the sides would be bins separating the kinds of potatoes.

The house they built, the lumber came from some hotel that was once in Terrebonne. They tore the hotel down. And he went down and got the lumber and built the house. I didn't even know there was a hotel at one time in Terrebonne.

Redmond was truly the farming community. Bend was really a foreign country then. Bend was mills, government and banks. So anyway, Grandpa was very private about his finances. And so he'd drive all this way to Bend to bank. He kept a very strange set of books. He never put any zeros down. He always dropped the last three zeros. So anything recorded in that book was in the thousands and so forth. And even that was coded. So nobody would know. So after he and Grandmother passed away and Mother went through some of this stuff no one could tell how much was really there.

That place was still leased out in the fifties. It was still a working farm but one of the neighbors was runnin' it after my grandfather past away. Grandma kept her turkeys and chickens and leased the ranch to the neighbor.

About two years ago we got the chance to save the lumber from that old barn when it was being torn down. And we're using it to build a new barn on our farm just east of Bend. I like the idea of saving the old to build the new.

As told to Ray Miao

Ray Clarno, b. 1929 in Walla Walla, WA. He came to live full time in Central Oregon in 1985 after a career with Carnation. He is currently working to have the "Badlands" declared a wilderness area and serving on two water quality boards. The eastern Oregon Clarno landmarks are named after his family.

Home Remedies

To Whiten Hands - Strained honey, 1 ounce; lemon juice, 1 ounce; cologne, 1 ounce. Mix and rub well into the hands at night, then wear a pair of large kid gloves, with the palms split for ventilation.

Vaucaire Bust Developer - The Vaucaire bust developer, an old formula said to be harmless, is made of five grains of liquid extract of imported galega, 5 grains of lacto-phosphate of lime, 5 grams of tincture of fennel and 200 grams of simple syrup. Take two soup spoons full in water before each meal. Drinking malt extracts at the same time is also advised by Dr. Vaucaire. It will probably be six weeks before a change is noticed.

Bed Bugs - Blue ointment and kerosene mixed in equal proportions and applied to bedsteads is an unfailing remedy for bedbugs, as a coat of whitewash is for the walls of a log house.

From the **Seattle Bride's Cookbook**

Old-Time Loggers

Leo Bishop

I came here to work for Brooks-Scanlon in 1930. For the first 12 years I worked in the box factory. In those days we made thousands and thousands of wooden boxes. Everything used boxes. Lettuce crates, orange crates, ammunition boxes.

They dried all their lumber outside. We had up to 40 million feet of lumber drying. It covered about 50 acres. We had no fences, no guards, kids played out there, and smoked out there and we never had a fire. I can't remember much vandalism. It always amazed me. This lumber was all piled by hand. Green lumber piled up about 18 or 20 feet. Most of it was piled by Scandinavian teamsters. And how they did it, I don't know. They had a jack and it would shoot that lumber up there. Somebody on top would catch it and pile it. It came down the same way. It was all moved by horses or a little narrow gage railroad with a gas engine.

All the teamsters wore black hats. I don't know why, but they all wore black hats. Sort of like a Quaker hat. But those Scandinavians sure worked hard and chewed lots of snooze (chewing tobacco).

All the timber was cut with crosscut saws. Two men to a team. They cut all the limbs with axes. Those timber fallers treated their axes just like you'd treat your watch. You'd better not touch that ax without their permission.

After they fell their trees they had a man with a team of horses that did the bunching. He tried to put the logs in groups of two, three or four. After all the logs were bunched, the teamsters would come along and run the high wheels right over the bunch and pick up the front end so it wouldn't drag. Then they'd bring 'em into the landing. The landing was always next to the railroad track. Here they had a couple of hookers. And they'd hook on each end of a log and pull it up onto the flat car.

All the lumber came on railroad cars. They used the Deschutes River above their mills for their ponds. And the train would dump their logs in the river and they'd float down to the mills. Years later when the company decided to get out of the river, it was my job to get all the logs out of the river and dredge it. And we took logs out of the bottom of the river that we estimated had been there 30 years and were just as sound as the day they were cut.

In the old days the mills burned all their bark, slab and sawdust. They kept enough out to power their own generators. Their burners were about 30 feet in diameter, 150 feet high and lined with firebrick. Then there was a conveyer that would go up about 50 feet and dump inside this big burner. That thing was burnin' 24 hours a day. The top was covered with a huge screen and you could see the sparks comin' out of there at night for miles.

In 1943 I went to work on the steel gang. The steel gang consisted of 19 men. Our job was to lay track for the railroads into the woods, pull it up when they finished logging in an area, then re-lay the track to open up the next stand. The boss was a guy in a white hat named "Paul Bunyon." He drank whiskey all night and worked us to death all day. We tried to pick up a quarter of a mile of steel one-day and lay it the next.

One day I was operating the steel rig and the brake man forgot to set the brake on one of the steel cars. It started right down over the hill. I yelled to the foreman and we unhooked the steam locomotive and all 19 of us climbed on chasin' that load of steel down the mountain. It was crazy as anything you ever saw in the movies. We knew our steel was goin' for the main line, and there was a locomotive and a string of cars comin' out. We were just horrified. The darn thing was so heavy that it made every curve, broke through the switch, went on the main line and stopped cold. We went out and hooked on to it and away we went.

You remember the old crooked road on Horse Ridge? The next time you go over the main highway on Horse Ridge, look over to the right. There's an old crooked road with lots of horseshoe bends. In the wintertime it was very dangerous with ice. Of course on Friday afternoon everybody would work hard and try to get in early. So here they come, just a sailin' down Horse Ridge. Old Ed was drivin' all by himself. He come around one of these corners and hit a spot of ice and over he went. All four wheels were up in the air spinning. And the next carload of guys coming along behind him saw Ed up on top of the car with a crescent wrench. And one guy said, "Ed, what are you doin'?" And Ed replied, "There'll never be a better time to tighten these loose bolts."

The old-time logger was something special. I really had a soft spot in my heart for them.

As told to Gretchen Williver
COCC Oral History Tapes 1977

Leo Bishop, b. 1913 in Wisconsin came to Central Oregon when he was nine years old. He worked for Brooks-Scanlon for 47 1/2 years before retiring.

George Alvin Cyrus

George Alvin Cyrus, known as Alvin, learned water witching in 1942, watching Homer Alexander, a hired hand. The forked willow stick never worked for Alvin so he used baling wire rods to "dowse."

Once Cyrus, Clyde Dahl and Perry Hereford, then historical sites chairman for the Deschutes County Historical Society, went to an old burial site near O'Neil to re-fence and mark it for Society records. Alvin had taken the wire with him because he had noticed when exploring for water on his farm that the wire reacted over spots where he had buried animals and he figured it would respond over graves.

He was glad he had it along that day as he felt he'd obtained some significant information. He estimated the man buried there had been about 5'2" tall, and was in the ground to a depth of four and a half feet because his divining rod bobbed four and a half times. Further, contends Cyrus, the grave runs north and south instead of the traditional east-west, so that on Judgment Day, Lark Weaver will rise and face north! Weaver was a homesteader in the Crooked River valley.

Excerpted from an interview by Martha Stranahan for
The Redmond Spokesman

George Alvin Cyrus b. 1907 in Cloverdale. He located several irrigation wells for neighbors using his water witching talents. He was recognized as a knowledgeable sheepman.

Small Town Stories

Coming together is a beginning;
Keeping together is progress;
Working together is success.

Henry Ford

It Was Just a Little Town

Phyllis (Gillispie) and Stan Sturza

"Redmond was just a little town," said Phyllis Sturza who has lived there since 1936 and her husband, Stan, who came to stay in 1939. How little was it?

Phyllis said she ran away from home when she was a little girl but nobody went to look for her cause everybody knew everybody including her, which meant nobody knew she was running away, so there wasn't any need to look for her! Besides, she wasn't big enough to get very far. And on top of that, she was the daughter of Bob Gillispie, the policeman. Ultimately she was "found" by a man who saw her on the street and asked what she was doing. The story she told was that she was looking for her mother who had gone to a movie. So the nice man bought her ice cream, then took her home, ending her big adventure.

Stan said that across the street from where Sully's is now there was a hardware store and there were ledges around it where the old guys in town, one of whom was his grandpa, liked to sit and whittle and talk and spit. "If you went downtown," he said, "and you didn't have any money, and you needed a nickel to get an ice cream, you'd just go over there and one of those old guys would give you a nickel and you could get an ice cream." That's how little the town was.

Stan started rodeoing professionally when he was about 14. He rode bareback horses and bulls and bulldogs. He'd get off school on Friday, go to a rodeo and not come back until late Sunday night. Why did he do it? "Because the people I was around did it, and I enjoyed it, and you got to travel all over the United States."

"I never had any serious accidents," he added. "I just had my back broke and arm broke and hand broke."

As told to Lorna Cerenzia

Stan Sturza performed and won many awards at the Sisters Rodeo. Stan and Phyllis live in Redmond.

The Scale of Things and The Times are Changing

Vadabell (Dodson Williams) Brumblay

Bend was just a small town center when I was a child in the 1920s. We lived south of the location of Chan's restaurant, in an area called Carroll Acres, after the Carroll family. Parrell Road was initially Parallel Road because it was parallel to Highway 97. However, it was converted to Parrell to make it easier to pronounce and to conform to the way most people said it anyway. Murphy Road, which was way outside the city limits then, was originally called Golf Course Road. Only one family lived south of Golf Course Road. That was really out of town!

In the spring, owners herded their sheep down Parrell Road to avoid the traffic on Highway 97. From there they journeyed as far as China Hat Road, where they got back on Highway 97 for a short time until they could herd the sheep toward the mountains for summer pasture.

As I child I went initially to the Carroll Acres School which was located where Cascade Gardens is now. In fact the white building there is one of the two original school buildings. Bend High then is where the current Bend-LaPine School District Offices are now, near the new library and what was then, the new post office. When the post office was built on the corner of Franklin and Wall Streets in the 1930s, it was most certainly the grandest structure in Bend.

One of the streets downtown wasn't fit for girls and women to be seen on. That was Bond Street, which had lots of pool halls on it. My father, Les Dodson, admonished my sister and me, "You just don't go on that street!" He also told us we couldn't go to the Pleasant Ridge Grange Hall because of the drunken behavior of some of the attendees, which earned it the name of Cuckoo Ridge Grange Hall.

The other Grange halls were o.k. They were our social and political centers and most of the families of the Oregon Pioneers, like my parents, went there frequently. While the interiors of the Granges were pretty plain, they had lots of conveniences including cots for sleepy children. There was a dance floor and raised stage for the various 4-5 piece bands, which played everything from country to the new jazz and swing music. Admission to the dances at Carroll Acres was 10 cents.

Life for most of us in Bend was based upon traditional farming. While some residents closer to town had more modern conveniences like iceboxes, we used the cellar under the back porch for our food storage. Mother put milk in a box with a cloth over it and a pan of water underneath. The cloth would siphon the water over the box to keep the milk cool and moist. We kept vegetables in the cellar to preserve them, kept apples in barrels just as they were, and used shelves for the fruits we bought and canned.

Dad had Jersey cows, and we milked the cows, cooled the milk, bottled it and capped each glass bottle with a little tabbed cardboard seal. After that, my mother, (Elnora “Dutch” Roberts Dodson) and I delivered our milk all over Bend. Our “milk wagon” was the family sedan with the back seat removed. Mother drove and I ran into each establishment with their milk order. They watched for me so they could put their milk up right away. If they didn’t, it would freeze in the winter and pop the cap off, or sour in the summer.

I have seen nothing but a change in the scale of this city and plan to see lots more. It’s not the same place it was when I was a child, but despite the growth, people are still really friendly here, and I think it’s exciting to watch the change.

As told to Karen Goodman & Shinann Earnshaw

Vadabell (Dodson) Brumblay, b. 1920 in Bend, Oregon. She attended schools in the Tumalo and Bend area. She worked as a bookkeeper in her husband’s business and she continues to live in Bend.

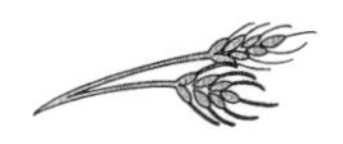

Everett (Bud) Van Matre

My father, Willis Van Matre was born before the Civil War and was 61 when I was born in 1919, the youngest of 6 children. Two were born in Missouri, two were born in Nebraska and then two of us were born in Oregon. It was at that point my mother Caroline told Dad that we were never going to move to another state. Every time we moved there were two more and the family was too big now!

We had one movie theatre in Redmond. It only showed silent movies until around 1927 or 1928. They would show the picture and then flash the words across the screen. Tom Mix was a big star then. Every Saturday morning the theatre would run one episode of a serial and it took 6 or 8 weeks to get this one story over with. We rode our horse into town, tied it to the hitch rack right across Main Street about half a block from the theatre, and it would have to stand there until the movie was over.

As told to Clara Varcoe-Lasher

Everett Van Matre, was born in Redmond in 1919 and was raised on a farm north of town. He owned and operated Van Matre Oil Company until the late 1980s. He was active in baseball and football. His father was on the first board of the Deschutes County Fair.

Porter "Mack" McKinley Houk

One summer we visited my brother, Fred, who had a Ford garage in Redmond. I really liked the area and told him I would like to move, but I would have to have a salary of $175 a month to match what I was currently making. The next May he came by and said he needed someone to take care of his books, and asked me to move over.

I went to work with my brother in his garage that was about 50 feet from the corner of Forest, on Main Street. We had only a one-gallon gas hand pump and a 550-gallon storage tank under the sidewalk. One year I pumped 50,000 gallons of gas out with that one-gallon pump. That was a lot of hand pumping! In 1924, after my brother's wife and nephew were killed in a car wreck, he lost interest in the garage but I kept it going until we sold it in 1927.

As told to Don Ellis
Courtesy of the Redmond Historical Commission

Redmond's Justice of the Peace

Donald Ellis

It was 1943 when my wife Dale and I arrived in Redmond. We had been living in Lemmon, South Dakota where I had practiced dentistry since 1929, but times were rough because of the war, and when money is scarce people ignore their teeth unless they're really hurting.

We arrived in April and I went to work at Camp Abbot, which is now Sunriver. That drive got kind of tiresome, so I switched to the Redmond Air Base and managed base supplies until the war was over.

I went to work for the county and along about 1953 I got to thinking that I should run for Justice of the Peace because the incumbent had an alcohol problem. I filed as a Republican. I got the Republican vote and a portion of the Democratic vote because the guy in office was a drunk.

When the general election rolled around I was elected for a 6-year term. I didn't know what I was doin' half the time, but after a while it got kind of interesting and I managed o.k. because the Justice of the Peace only handled minor problems like drunk driving, speeding, running stop signs and things like that.

There were a lot of drunk driving cases back then too. Sometimes they'd lose their license, and I never knew how they would react when that happened. One truck driver just wanted to get the whole thing over with and be on his way. I warned him he might lose his license if he was caught drivin' drunk again. He went right out and did the same thing over again, so I took his license, and he just sat there and cried.

Another driver was picked up for not having a license. In fact, he'd never applied for one. People who couldn't read or write didn't realize that you could still get one if you could read the traffic signs. Of course, you also had to be able to read the speed limits. He and I had a talk about that and I told him to go down to the DMV and see what they had to say, then come back in to see me. Two days later he came back with his license in hand and darn near flew through the door.

For twenty-four years I served as Justice of the Peace in Redmond. I issued citations, heard a lot of cases and performed about 300 marriage ceremonies before I retired. Guess it's a good thing I got tired of pulling teeth, 'cause I enjoyed my second career a whole lot more than the first.

As told to Julie Ross

Donald L. Ellis was born in Wisconsin in 1903 and moved to Redmond in 1943. He has been an agricultural extension agent as well as a Justice of the Peace. He has lived at the same address since 1943.

Moonshine
Darwin Clark

Back in the prohibition days I was a kid, but I knew what went on. The desert clear out to Silver Lake was full of little shacks where the stuff was bubbling... out there with the jackrabbits and coyotes.

One still near Tumalo kept the "revenooers" busy a long time trying to figure out where it was made and how it was peddled.

The blacksmith on the hill was a good Samaritan and each Saturday afternoon he delivered a load of firewood to the church. His open forge was in front of his house. Inside the forge he would chat with customers and clang on his anvil.

The forge chimney piped the boiler smoke into the air. Brew was stashed beneath the church firewood, plucked out by dancers for the Saturday night fling at the local hall and the worshippers never knew.

One day a "revenooer" idly tugged on a thong and opened a trapdoor to the still below. The smithy fled and authorities arrested and sent to prison his loyal purveyor who served his time and never "squealed."

Excerpted from an interview by Martha Stranahan for
The Redmond Spokesman

Darwin Clark, 1923 - 1999. His parents were early homesteaders in the Tumalo area. After a career in forestry and some farming he was the Deschutes County appraiser. He is well known for telling interesting stories about this country.

Photo courtesy of Joyce Gribskov

Leave Me, or I'll Haunt You

Bernardine Shaw Lowery

My parents homesteaded in the Tumalo area in 1920 or 21. Dad was a ditch rider, which meant he adjusted the head gates to tell how much water goes out to each person. Doctors were scarce in Central Oregon then, so my father sent my mother to the hospital in McMinnville where I was born in February of 24. Mom came back by the train, which went as far as Shaniko. Father met her there and they spent the night at the Shaniko Hotel. Seventy-two years later my youngest son was married in that same hotel.

One of my earliest memories is of the trip we took to Yellowstone National Park in a Model T Ford. We had quilts in the back for warmth and there was a built-in trunk on the front of the car, which held our pans, cooking utensils, and a set of tin plates and cups. There weren't any McDonalds then, or even any paper plates. When it was time to eat we stopped and cooked our meals beside the road.

Mother had gotten dentures just before we left and she still had some sore spots in her mouth. She took her dentures out each evening and put them in a cup, which for some unknown reason she sat on top of the car where the ribs went across it to hold the top on tight. One morning we took off with the teeth still up there in that cup and evidently drove quite some distance before anyone realized it. When we stopped they were still up there, so she retrieved them, washed 'em, put 'em in her mouth and we went on our way again.

A second vivid childhood memory is of the windstorm that took place in 34 or 35. Although the wind had come up, my folks didn't realize how bad it would get and let me walk to a birthday party. On the way home one tree went down in front of me and another one went down behind me. That wind made a clean swipe from down on the Metolius River up to about Squaw Creek and then began to peter out.

Photo courtesy of Joyce Gribskov

In 1940 I married Jack Lowery. At the time he lived at the Brooks-Scanlon camp about sixty miles east of Bend. Later we moved to Sisters where we raised our three children, Jack, Buster and Susie. After the three of them finished their education, I went back to the books myself and got my nursing degree.

When Sisters needed a new cop, they hired a man whose name I won't mention. He had an ambulance, which he used to cart us old people back and forth. Well, one day he came into Redmond with a patient and his blankets were dirty because he had been hauling garbage in that ambulance. That was more than this nurse could handle and I told everybody who would listen, "If you ever let him pick me up, I'll haunt you! Just leave me lay along the road." As it turned out, that incident was the catalyst for starting our ambulance station. A lot of us worked on getting it established and it has become an important service in the Sisters area.

As told to Carol J. B. Illinik

Bernardine (Shaw) Lowery, b.1925. She married at the early age of 15 after attending the Plainview school. She was in one of the first classes to graduate from the COCC nursing program in the 1960s.

824 Newport Avenue, 1920s.

Flying Teeth and Rolling Planes

Don Hinman

I was born in 1922 at 824 Newport Avenue in Bend. The house is still there though it looks different now, but that's true for the rest of the neighborhood as well. Houses and grocery stores are what I remember most.

Boardman's Groceries was on the corner of 10th and Newport. When you first walked in that store in the wintertime the smell of kerosene hit you like a big blast, but that wasn't unusual in those days as kerosene heaters were common. Carter's grocery was two blocks up the street. He had a bigger stock, but we really didn't go there very much.

Leo Herbring's pretty nice grocery store was on the corner of Harmon and Newport. He had a freezer and ice cream and a lot of things that the other stores didn't have. He even had a cement block out in front with a gas pump sittin' on it. I'm pretty sure he pumped the gas, but he didn't wash your windshield.

My folks went downtown to Erickson's Groceries, which was across from the Tower Theater. Art Erickson would come by the house in the morning, take your grocery order and bring it back in the afternoon. His store was cash on one side and credit on the other. It wouldn't surprise me if there were people around who still owe him money on food they bought years ago.

We had a neighbor who always walked by our west windows on his way to work at the post office. One day we saw him go by, then come right back in a little bit. We wondered why, but soon learned that when he got down to the Drake Park footbridge he sneezed or coughed and spit his dentures into the river. My gosh, he was upset. Anyway, the Fire Department or somebody came out and retrieved them so he was all right after that.

Newport was rough and unpaved back in 1935 and there wasn't much traffic on it. One spring day that was half rain and half sun, I heard a different noise, looked out the front window, and saw an airplane rollin' down the street. I don't know just where it hit the ground, but I know that when he got across from us he hit a power pole with his left wing and ground looped. He wasn't hurt, but both wings on the left side were gone. The pilot was Ted Barber, a local aviation pioneer. Forty years later, the company I was workin' for sent me down to Orovada, Nevada to learn about irrigation pumping. When I saw some airplanes sitting around and ran into a guy named Barber, I had to ask him, "Did you ever ride your airplane on Newport Avenue?" And he had. It was the same fella'.

Newport Avenue was a nice part of town to grow up in back then. And it still is, but I don't recommend landing a plane there anymore.

As told to Ray Miao

Don Hinman, was born in Bend in 1922. He has lived in Redmond since 1946 and worked for Central Electric Co-op for 23 years before retiring. He was mayor of Redmond from 1959 to 1963.

The Great Spud Cellar Caper

Jerry Shepard

In thinking back on my growing up years on our farm in the Tumalo community, I am reminded of certain events, some of them happy and some of them sad. My father, Fred, was not always noted for artistic detail when it came to construction projects around the farm. This is not to say that what he built was not satisfactory, but rather that it was not yet ready for the Metropolitan Museum.

For many years, starting in the mid-1920s, Dad milked ten to fifteen cows and sold the separated cream to the Co-op Creamery in Redmond. By the 1940s Pop decided to upgrade the dairy industry on the farm to GRADE A. This move required the building of a new facility. Dad and other local farmers, including a neighbor, Joe Henry, sat down and drew up a suggested plan. In due time, this cow palace was built. It was constructed in the 40s and still stands today.

Another engineering endeavor did not meet with the same success. I am referring to the ill-fated "Spud Cellar Caper." In the 1930s when the potato harvest was due, the growers prepared for storing the Deschutes Netted Gem (now called Russets). Most farmers in the area dug a long trench about 24 inches deep. The spuds were emptied into the trench and covered with straw and topped with several inches of soil. One big drawback to this system was it was cold, hard and nasty work; thus alternatives were explored. Some neighbors began building permanent potato cellars. It was under these circumstances that my dad decided to create a masterpiece. He "rode off like a knight errant" in pursuit of this dream.

First he chose a site across from our home. Then Leonard Truax brought in his caterpillar and dug a pit. It was to have two entrances so a truck could drive in one end and out the other. Dad chose lodge pole pine for the building material which meant that he and one of his sons had to go into the mountains and hand-saw 8 to 10 inch diameter trees, hoist the logs onto the truck and haul them to the construction site. Somehow, probably because I was off to college, I missed out on this prodigious task.

Then a concrete foundation was laid upon which to rest the split logs. To keep them from slipping off the footings, old mower sickle guards were imbedded in the concrete, pointing upward. The half-log had a one-inch hole drilled into the bottom to fit over the mower guard. This turned out to be a faulty scientific engineering error.

In due time, construction began on this behemoth. The walls were erected, crossbeams were installed, rafters were raised into place and so it went. Some sort of a roof was laid over the rafters and then straw was laid down for insulation. Finally several inches of soil was deposited on top of the straw. Hollow doors were filled with juniper needles for insulation and were finally put into place.

During the fall season in 1948, load after load of Netted Gem tubers found their way to the cellar for safe keeping. Then over the Christmas holidays, it was discovered that some structural deterioration had taken place on the northwest quadrant. A few timbers had slipped causing daylight to become evident and throwing light onto the unsuspecting spuds. Dad inspected the situation and determined that for the time being the cellar would hold up.

In the ensuing weeks the potatoes were sorted, and trucked off to market. As summer approached it became evident that serious maintenance would be necessary. During the spring, more daylight was seen. More beams and columns were installed to shore up the structure.

Leonard Truax returned with his caterpillar to make repairs. He gently moved the soil against the side wall. Dad acted as overseer from a vantage point 10 to 15 feet up on the roof. I was standing on the south side observing. About five minutes into the job a faint cracking sound was heard, a sound that quickly became louder and more ominous.

Dad, sensing that all was not going well, headed for the lower section of the roof and as he did so, it swayed, hesitated, and then collapsed. Pop just made it to safety before it came down. The walls collapsed inward. Dad had worked so hard and put so much time and effort into the project that the look on his face was one of utter dismay. Surely it must have been one the lowest points in his farming career.

Jerry Shepard, was born on the family farm near Tumalo at the beginning of the great Depression. He had a teaching career in the Salem school system for nearly thirty years. He is currently retired in Madras.

Keith and Aileen (Gregg) Ferguson

During the years we attended Redmond Union High School we were let out of school for a week or two to pick up the many acres of Netta Gem potatoes. This, of course, was before potato combines were used. They were dug by a machine pulled by horses and later tractors and left laying on top of the ground. The picker either wore a belt to which gunny (burlap) sacks were attached and drug along the row as the spuds were picked up by hand and put into the sack. An alternative, easier-on-the-back method was to use wire bushel baskets. Two of them made up a 60-pound sack of potatoes.

Aileen's parents couldn't afford to send her to business college because of the Depression so she worked in the school office for two class periods each day. That was her training for later working first in the Production Credit Office, which gave loans to farmers, and then for many years as a secretary for the Redmond School District.

As told to Clara Varcoe-Lasher

Keith, b. 1923 in South Dakota and Aileen (Gregg) Ferguson, b. 1921 in Shaniko, Oregon both moved to Central Oregon in the 1930s. They met at Redmond High School. Aileen's great grandfather Crates was a French Canadian fur trader and explorer. They currently live in Terrebonne.

Kem Scorvo

My grandparents had cows and my parents had cows. I've been told that one day, not long after I had learned to walk, I got away from my mother out in the barn while the cows were all in getting milked. I walked underneath all of the cow's bellies as they were standing there. They were all watching this very small child walk under one cow after another, and each, in turn, stood stark still as I walked beneath her. None of them ever did a thing. They just stood there.

In those days Redmond was a very small town and you couldn't get away with anything. Redmond was a town full of mothers. And if you did anything bad, by the time you got home your parents would know all about it.

As told to Joyce Gribskov

Kem Scorvo b. 1946 at St. Charles Hospital, Bend. She attended school in Redmond, moved away and returned in 1988. Kem works as an RN in the emergency room at St. Charles Medical Center.

Helen O'Brien

I shall never forget when we first moved into the "Tar Papered" shack in the middle of the Brooks-Scanlon mill yard in 1933. From then until they did away with the workhorses in the early 50s, my Dad was the barn boss. Those draft horses hauled lumber on small rail tracks down to the green chain. They also pulled the water wagon, which was used to keep the dust down on the dirt roads that encircled the mill yard. Dad was responsible for doctoring the horses as well as keeping the barn sanitary.

It was up to the drivers of the horses to brush and curry them both before and after they were used. If the drivers didn't take good care of them and treat the horses with respect, he fired them on the spot!

Written by Helen O'Brien

Helen O'Brien, b. 1926 in Carso, MO. Her father homesteaded in the Agency Plains above Madras when she was 9 months old. She married Tom O'Brien, raised 3 children and ran a restaurant in Seattle.

Anna Eskew

John Perry donated the land for the Terrebonne Cemetery in 1918. It's a little bigger than three acres and for many years the Ladies' Pioneer Club took care of it. Many times Evelyn and I measured out lots when the snow was knee deep. Sometimes it'd be hard to find the lots that they had bought that they wanted to be buried in. And we'd have to scoop snow and scoop snow to find the closest one we could get to, to line 'em up. Every spring we all went down to clean the cemetery. We had to rake it all by hand and burn it down there. Once when we were doing that we caught the telephone pole on fire. Three years ago we gave it up. We just got too old to paddle around in all that snow.

As told to Julie Ross

Anna Eskew, b. 1915 moved to Cline Falls in 1935. She spent her life as a homemaker raising a family. She has lived in Terrebonne since 1942.

Shepherds of Sheep and Boys

Vincent J. Rosengarth

'Tis a fortunate person who has an extra set of parents and in the 50s, my younger brother and I were lucky enough to be in that category. Dave and Caroline Clifford lived down Butler Market Road from us. He, a tall, slim immigrant from Ireland was a sheep man, while his wife was his opposite. She, considerably heavier and shorter, worked two jobs including ironing clothing for other people. Our special relationship began when they gave us an Austrian shepherd. During the cold and snowy winter months their house became our refuge. Caroline was a wonderful cook and her specialties were various cakes and sweets.

With a player piano in her living room, a complete library of National Geographic magazines and a great encyclopedia set to pour over, we spent many a cold winter day in their house sipping hot chocolate or bottled Sprite. Though Caroline's fingers were short and chubby they seemed to glide over the keyboard as she played the piano remarkably well. My brother Richard and I were company for Dave who didn't work during the winter months.

The other nine months of the year he was away from home out with the flocks. Several months after their birth the owner would split his flocks into smaller flocks and send them to government grazing areas. The sheepherder would attend the flock on horseback with several dogs. He controlled those dogs with voice and hand commands. We were not allowed to pet or play with those working dogs.

During a fantastic summer we would be permitted to spend four or five weekends with them. That Irishman was delighted to get our help for all he had to do then was drive the truck. We loaded and unloaded the water troughs, pumped water, put out the salt blocks and feed. Dave loved to listen to Rich and I sing. The big old dual wheeled truck didn't have a radio. Dave was simply in heaven when we sang as he drove. His favorite was:

"He's got the whole world in his hands,
He's got the whole wide world in his hands."

Early Saturday afternoons was a special treat when we were camped near a town. That allowed Caroline time to drive back to camp without the ice cream melting. It was wrapped up in newspaper as an insulator and tied with string. They only had a small refrigerator; it had to be consumed immediately. She always bought two half gallons. One for her and Dave and of course the second for Rich and I.

Yaa hoo, the very best weekend of the year was at the end of summer. That was three or four days in which all the sheep were rounded up, separated and put into corrals. I enjoyed helping with that but was saddened when the lambs were put into tractor-trailer rigs and shipped to market. The old ewes were herded back to the ranch to start the process all over.

Dave and Caroline were far from rich financially. However, our first jobs were washing her car, cutting the grass and various other projects. We were given that special something for our birthdays and Christmas. I'm positive she worked numerous hours simply to provide us with those gifts. My only regrets are that my career didn't allow me to visit and thank them more, and secondly that I didn't write this letter to them personally thirty years ago while they were still alive.

One winter George had brought home a Canadian Honker (goose) which he had shot. He went hunting frequently in those days. George had shot this 20-23 pound Honker out of the sky, which landed near a road in the snow. As he approached his trophy, the bird came alive. Hissing, wheezing and flapping his wings and running toward him. George became completely mystified. Turning his double-barreled shotgun around he cuffed the goose with the butt end. Woo-laa, dinner at last. Proudly he brought it home to Mother to cook. Not knowing exactly how to prepare and cook such a bird, she summoned Caroline. She cooked it in some kind of wine. Her meals were never served without some type of dessert. After spending the majority of the day preparing the feast, she simply delivered it to our house. That was typical of Caroline's generosity.

Vincent J. Rosengarth was born in Bend in 1946. He was raised on a small farm on Butler Market Road. He retired in 1985 after a career with the U.S. Navy.

Gwen Dent

Terrebonne used to be called Hillman. There are a couple of stories about how it became Terrebonne though nobody seems to know which is true. One story floatin' around was that Hill and Harriman were the guys who helped build the railroad and Hillman was a combination of their names. But then a man named Hillman was selling land around here that didn't belong to him. The people didn't want their town named after this crook and so they changed the name to Terrebonne, which means good earth.

When we went to buy the house down on F Street we went to the lawyer. When he said, "The house is in Hillman," my husband told him, "I'm not buyin' a house in Hillman. I want it in Terrebonne." "Don't worry," the lawyer replied, "you're still buyin' a place in Terrebonne; it just says Hillman on your deed." I wonder if people buyin' today still have Hillman listed on their deeds.

The Good Earth Day Parade is in Terrebonne. It's just a parade. I think it's the shortest parade in Oregon.

As told to Julie Ross

Gwen Dent was born in Portland, Oregon in 1922. She moved to Central Oregon in 1940 and has lived in the same location in Terrebonne for 36 years.

Ron Hall

I worked with my dad, Gordon Hall, when he had the radio shop on Wall Street in downtown Bend. He had been a radioman on a submarine during WW I. There was only one radio station in Bend and to get the big Portland stations you had to have a really high and pretty good sized antenna. Radios were pretty large then with the consoles being about 3 feet wide and 4 feet high, but they weren't very strong when it came to pulling in the signal. Once when my dad demonstrated a radio to someone he took 6 tubes out of the 18-tube radio and it kept playing. The manufacturers used to put lots of tubes in them so people thought they were getting something better.

Dad also had a sound truck for broadcasting. He used the truck for all the announcers at the baseball games, the Bend Elks, the Lava Bears and rodeos and would even go around town using the truck for advertising.

As told to Joyce Gribskov

Ron Hall, born in 1927 at St. Charles Hospital, lived in Bend until 1945 when he joined the Navy. He lives in California, but summers in Bend. The family is directly related to Dr. Lyman Hall, a signer of the Declaration of Independence.

Mervin & Lena Sampels

In 1937 Mervin and Lena Sampels purchased approximately ten acres of land from Nels and Lillian Anderson for $500. With their four children they spent weekends working on their new home site. During the week they lived at a Brooks-Scanlon logging camp where Mervin worked. By the summer of 1938 they had completed enough of their two-story, three-bedroom home so they could move in. They planted many of the trees that still stand on the property, which they sold in 1947. Today that land is occupied by the Bend Welcome Center and the Oregon Department of Transportation office. Mervin Sampels Road, which is located off Highway 97 just south of Empire, was later named for the former owner.

Excerpted from a tribute to the Sampels family by the Bend Chamber.

How A Broken Axle Brought the Rich and Famous Our Way

Roblay McMullin and Eliza Gallois

I met Roblay McMullin and Eliza Gallois during the 60s, when I was making denim skirts for Eliza, as well as patchwork skirts for the guests at Roblay's Lake Creek Lodge. While I measured and fitted, the two women told me these stories over and over at my request.

Their sojourn in Central Oregon began in the 20s, shortly after World War I. Eliza and her husband John were driving up the old Dalles-Klamath Falls road and broke an axle south of Crescent. The Coombs Garage (now Bob Thomas Chevrolet-Cadillac) towed them in and they took refuge in the Pilot Butte Inn across the street to await the parts needed to repair their car.

John, an avid fisherman, asked the mechanic where he could find the best fishing in the area and was directed to the Metolius. One day on that beautiful river was all it took for him to become so enchanted with the area that he decided to buy some land and build a summer home there. That was difficult to do because almost every acre of homesteaded land was mortgaged, so when he located a three-plus acre plot on the river he bought it outright.

Eliza went with him the next time he fished and they outlined with rocks what would become "House-on-Metolius" in the manner of "Stratford-on- Avon." She left a blank area where the windows looking out onto Mt. Jefferson were to go and piled rocks where the big fireplace should be built. Before leaving they ordered $500 worth of building materials from Montgomery Ward's and hired Henry Nelson to build them the house to be ready for the next summer.

Sometime later John and Eliza were traveling in Europe when they met and made friends with the owners of the Lorillard Tobacco Company. When that couple later divorced, John and Eliza persuaded Bertha Ronalds, the wife, to come to the Metolius and build an estate with some of her settlement money. She purchased 160 acres, which is now Metolius Meadows, and the Hansen Resort, which was across the street. Eliza got her brother, Bud McMullin and his young wife Roblay to come take care of Bertha, who was ailing, and nurse her back to health.

When Bertha tired of the quiet lifestyle and returned to the east, she left the land to Bud and Roblay who then sold Metolius Meadows and re-built Hansen's Resort into Lake Creek Lodge. The price of the land sale was $37,000, and according to Roblay, the old Brussels schoolmaster oils she left on the walls in Bertha's house (because she didn't like big pictures of barnyards) each sold for that sum at a later date.

Lake Creek Lodge had become, and continued to be, a popular place for the rich and the famous to vacation, year after year, and feast on Roblay's special menus which were always the same for each day of the week. There was salmon on Friday, chicken on Saturday, and steak and polenta on Sunday nights, with the same side dishes and dress-ings, all created by Roblay. You could count on it.

When John died after World War II, Eliza sold House-on-Metolius to Eleanor Bechen, co-founder of the Pine Tavern, who ran it as a "bed and breakfast" type inn, which actually served dinner instead of a morn-ing meal. Much to the displeasure of Eliza, Eleanor changed the name to House on the Metolius. Though there was a period when it served as a retreat house, it is a guesthouse again and is now owned by Kim Lundgren, who grew up in the house next door.

Lake Creek Lodge was eventually purchased by Camp Tamarack owners Margaret Lumpkin, Lisa Taubman and Velda Burst, and others, and at the time of this writing, is on the market again.

With every sale and re-sale of these landmarks, a piece of interesting local history becomes more difficult to trace and it seems worthwhile to record this information while there are still people around who can provide first hand accounts of their origin.

By Harriet Langmas

Harriet Langmas was born in 1932 in Portland, Oregon. She moved to Central Oregon in 1956. Her varied careers include teaching journalism, fashion designing, teaching piano and lecturing on cruise ships. She has been actively involved in PEO, AAUW, CO Symphony Society and Oregon Literacy Council.

Arthur Sproat

My grandparents had the first dairy at Fort Rock. My dad came from the valley to find work there and that's where he met and married my mom. I was born in the old town of Fremont, which was right at the foot of the rock. All that's left of it now is the steppin' stones for the ladies to get on their horses and the Fremont wells.

My folks raised rye to feed their cattle. They had a 110 foot well. That's the way they watered their cattle. The watering trough was a hewn out log, which was up in the air so the cattle wouldn't tear it down. They pumped the water out of the well by windmill.

As told to Clara Varcoe-Lasher

Arthur Sproat was born in Fort Rock in 1923. He lived throughout the area including Sisters, the Brooks-Scanlon logging camps and Terrebonne. He worked in the timber industry as well as for the school district and the Deschutes County Fairgrounds. His grandfather, Henry Chapman, started the first dairy in the area.

Places of Interest

No matter where you go
Or what you do,
That's where you'll be
And what you'll do.

Fred Pigue

The Museum of Wonders

Frances Forbes Turner

There is a small gray stucco building on Division Street that has been used in recent years for a picture framing business, an espresso shop and a coffee/lunch house. Newcomers are prone to look at it and question the architectural taste of the builder, that is until they understand what's behind it. Old time local residents know that it used to be a rock museum called the Museum of Wonders. Much of the collection it housed was gathered in the 1930s from the Forbes family homesteads, one of which was at Lost Creek near Glass Butte and one in Lake County.

When the walls of the building went up in 1936, pieces of black obsidian were pressed into the stucco before it was dry. On the roof, outlined in black obsidian are a crescent, a star and an Indian arrowhead. The builders, Lloyd and Bertha Forbes, lived with their family in a section built onto the shop. Their three children, Robert, Mary and Frances learned to turn lathes to help create lamps, furniture and other juniper wood novelties sold to tourists who stopped to see the rock collection and hear the geological history of each item.

Lloyd rigged up a saw in his shop to cut through the dull gray rocks called thundereggs to reveal their beautiful agate interiors. However, as spectacular as they were, it was the obsidian that the children liked the best because it reflected the sun's rays. Not all obsidian is black; some is opaque, having layers of blue, red and gold, with all their hues and tints. The most beautiful and scarce is the deep blue obsidian. Geologists told Mr. Forbes that he was the only person having some of these specimens. They also credited him with the discovery of certain variations of obsidian in this part of the world.

One of the most remarkable things in the Forbes collection was the petrified wood. There were entire logs of green agate showing knots and rings of growth. Some logs had green bark, or a beautiful fringe of black agate about a half inch thick.

When a violet-ray light was turned on above one display of gray rocks, they immediately took on beautiful colors of orchid, deep purple and green. One glowed a deep wine red and had silver stars in it. Yet when Mary placed a few of the other thundereggs or bits of petrified wood in the light, they remained the same color as before. When someone asked how she could tell the iridescent rocks from those that weren't, Mary laughed and said, "Just as farmer's children can tell a wheat field from an oat field, or Jerseys from Guernseys. It's all in getting used to it." The display became a favorite attraction for tourists who proclaimed this is surely a Museum of Wonders. The Museum operated until 1973.

Some of the rock gardens that surrounded the museum are still visible today - a colorful collection of tiny rock houses, rock bridges, rock archways and pathways of rock, as well as petrified wood.

As told to Barbara Baumgardner

Frances (Forbes) Turner was born in 1931 in Bend. She and her husband live in Madras. Mary Forbes, 1929-2000, had a long and honored career as a missionary and teacher.

The Family Before the Hollinshead Barn and Museum

By Laura Wonser

Dean Hollinshead was the youngest of William Henry and Ella May Hollinshead's three boys. The family moved to the La Pine area from Independence, Oregon when he was eight months old. A small cabin, owned by the Bogues, was their first home in Central Oregon which was also home to a lot of bears. One day Ella May was busy in the cabin when she heard a noise, turned and saw half of a brown bear hanging inside the window. At that point she was ready to return to Independence, but William calmed her down and boarded up the window and before long the country began to grow on her.

It was always a great place for the boys. They worked hard as they were growing up, but they had a lot of fun too. Like fishing. It was good in the Deschutes River and they'd hitch up the wagon and head on up to Pringle Falls where there were lots of fat Dolly Vardens laying around in the fishing holes. William Chester, the oldest boy could catch all the fish he wanted in just a few minutes with a cane pole.

Once Dean and Cecil, the middle brother, were riding in the wagon. Dean threw his lariat out trying to rope a stump. He never expected to make it, but he did. Not knowing what to do then, he tied his end of the rope to the end of his wagon seat. They were riding at a fast pace and when that rope tightened, the seat came off the wagon. Suddenly Cecil and Dean were sitting in the middle of the road and their dad didn't know why they had fallen off. They were soundly spanked.

Dean got his first Model T Ford in 1916. In 1924, when you heard someone call a road, "a good road," it required some explaining by today's standards. In the spring, "good" meant getting from Bend to La Pine in one day, if the mud wasn't too bad. In the winter it was a little slower. In the summer, it was "good" if the dust didn't get a foot deep as the Studebaker and Cadillac stages churned up and down the "highway."

Chet and Cecil, the two older brothers, bought the W.R. Riley's General Grocery Store in La Pine and later bought three freight trucks. Meanwhile, Dean got a job driving for Jess Hunsaker who owned the stageline and from this job he worked into the freighting business with his brothers.

In 1931 he married a young schoolteacher named Lily Hoard, who eventually kept the books for the company, as well as teaching school. In 1939 the two of them bought property on Jones Road in Bend where they had room for the good horses they both loved to ride. Lily organized the Red Rider's Saddle Club for young people who had their own horses. They dressed in red shirts and white hats and performed at fairs and Rim Rock play days. Both Dean and Lily were active in the Rim Rock Riding Club, helping with the outdoor breakfasts that raised money for the club, serving as officers and assisting with the general construction of the building and grounds.

Dean, along with Reub Long and Shorty Gustafson, also handled the horses for several movies that were made in Central Oregon. They can be seen in them driving stagecoaches or wrangling wild horses.

As time caught up with Dean and Lily, they reduced their holdings on Jones Road. They kept 16.5 acres for themselves and stayed until Dean's death in 1983. The property was then given to the Bend Park and Recreation Department to develop as a park and museum. Lily moved to a local retirement home where she lived until she died a few years later. The restored barn at Hollinshead Park is available to the public to rent for weddings and other special events. Dean and Lily's daughter, Sharron Rosengarth and her husband Tony, with the help of Bend Parks and Recreation, renovated the old Hollinshead Homestead House. It was finished as it was during the 1939 - 1949 time period.

Laura Lakin Wonser was born in Central Oregon. Her maternal great grandparents cofounded the town of Antelope. Laura married Dean Wonser in 1944 and operated the Bend dairy until 1970. It is now the roller rink on Greenwood Ave.

The First Sunriver Development Plan

By Brooke Snavely

Wade and Dorothy Collins and their twin sons Donald and Ronald came to Bend in 1948. They purchased the Gateway Tavern on Bond Street near the Shevlin-Hixon mill. After they had been in business about a year, the Elkhorn Cafe came up for sale and they bought it as well. Dorothy ran the restaurant while Wade managed the tavern. Eventually they sold the tavern and focused on the restaurant until they discovered a very interesting piece of property south of town was for sale.

In 1946, two years before the Collins' moved to the area and after World War II was over and the military installation at Camp Abbot closed down, the Bend Lodge of the Elks purchased that surplus property from the federal government. A few years later they put it up for sale. When they learned it was available, the Collins' struck a deal to buy it with the intention of establishing a restaurant and nightclub there. The year was 1953 and the $29,000 purchase price for Camp Abbot included the Great Hall, 365 acres surrounding it, and the entire river frontage from Harper Bridge to Col. Besson Bridge. To finance the deal the Collins' sold their Bend home on 10-acres and traded in a new Cadillac.

"We hired a man to manage the Elkhorn Cafe and moved out to Camp Abbot and started getting it ready to open," said Dorothy Collins. "To begin with, we built a big walk-in cooler and all the things needed to operate a restaurant. Then we got a liquor license and installed a nice bar in the lower room of the Great Hall. Wade planned on having dances on weekdays in a side room and big name bands for dances in the Great Hall on weekends."

Their plan was to offer three piece musical entertainment most weeknights and bring in big bands for major events. To do that they hired a piano player and a drummer, gave them room and board, and Wade joined them on the saxophone.

An Oregonian article dated July 19, 1953 stated: "The new owners plan extensive development of the property including tourist cabins, a trailer camp, picnic facilities and ultimately construction of stables for saddle horses and pack strings."

"It was a good idea," Dorothy Collins said, "but it wasn't the right time. People just didn't have the money to go to a place 15 miles out of town. We had a few customers but not enough for the restaurant to be profitable. There were some banquets and parties, but we were just losing money, so we closed it and went back to running the Elkhorn Cafe on Third Street again."

The Collins' lived at Sunriver for another two years until they sold the Sunriver property to the Hudspeth family in Prineville who ran cattle on it. Lee Evans, who married into the Hudspeth family, acquired the property in 1963 and researched various uses before selling it to John Gray in 1968. He developed Sunriver as it is known today.

Brooke Snavely has written for TV, radio, magazines and newspapers and contributed to four books since arriving in Bend in 1989. He and his wife, Katy Elliott, and their son, Hunter, live near Shevlin Park west of Bend.

Fly-Fishing in the 40s

Lloyd and Joanne Evans

My father began making flies because he liked to fish. At the time he was working at the mill and after word of what he was doing got around, he started making them for other people. That's how the business got started in 1936. We called it the Evans Fly Company and we were well known all over the Northwest.

Dad and I both did a lot of fishing. My mother loved to fly fish and my wife has her fishing rod now. Both of them loved to fish in Snow Creek, which is north of the Crane Prairie Reservoir. At that time it had lots of beautiful eastern brook trout in it.

In 1943 and 1944, my father and I took guide trips on the Deschutes River. We had a lot of clients from Southern California, mostly people wanting to fly fish. My partner and I would normally take them from Pringle Falls down to Big River Bridge, or from the Big River Bridge area down towards Sunriver. Most of the time the fishing was fabulous with the best being in the section from Pringle Falls to Big River Bridge. There were practically no roads to get in to that area then and the average fish was probably 16 to 24 inches. We did the whole trip for about $35 per person, which was quite a bit of money in those days.

As told to Sharon and Larry Snell

Lloyd Evans was born in Bend in 1927. He attended Allen School and Bend High and married Joanne in 1946. He owned Evans Fly Co. for 22 years and was a Chevron Oil distributor for 23 years. The Evans live in Bend.

It Was This Big!

John C. Veatch II

My dad was an avid fisherman. In 1935 he bought a cabin on Elk Lake because he liked to hunt and fish and help my grandfather with the cattle he grazed at Crane Prairie. In those days, there were rainbow trout in the lake, but some kind of worm started killing the fish. Eventually it got so bad they had to poison the lake and then they re-stocked it with eastern brook. That's mainly what it's been since then.

Before 1935 they took all the eggs from the rainbow trout and shipped them to New Zealand. That's how New Zealand got their start in the fishing industry. To harvest the fish, they put racks across the river to keep the fish from going on up to spawn. The fish would be hauled out of the racks. Of course, the river was closed to fishing then.

My dad was Chairman of the Fish Commission for 30 years here in Oregon. The Game Commission wanted to study the health of the fish and made arrangements with Dad to collect specimens for them. We'd catch fish, clean them and put their guts in quart jars which we sent to Portland.

The biggest fish I ever caught was 27" and 9 pounds. That's no fish story because I had it mounted.

As told to Shelley Palmer

John C. Veatch II was born in Portland in 1920. He moved to Central Oregon in 1987 but vacationed at Elk Lake every summer since 1923. He practiced law in Portland for 30 years and currently lives in Bend.

Homemade Ginger Beer

2 cups sugar
6 quarts boiling water
1 compressed yeast cake
2 lemons
1 tablespoon Jamaica ginger
1 tablespoon cream of tartar

Put the sugar, thinly peeled rind and juice of the lemons into a large bowl or pan, pour the boiling water over them and let stand until lukewarm. Dissolve the yeast in two tablespoons of lukewarm water, add to the first mixture with the cream of tartar and ginger and stir all thoroughly together. Bottle, cork and tie down or wire the corks. Lay the bottles on their sides, set aside in a cool place for at least three days before using.
The corks must be thoroughly fastened down, otherwise the working ginger will force them out. Two tablespoons of ground ginger may be substituted for the ginger extract if desired but the extract makes a stronger flavored drink and one a little clearer in appearance.

This is the old-fashioned stone-bottled ginger beer of grandmother's day.

The Book of Cookery, *1931, Manning Publishing Co., Chicago, IL, page 38.*

To Save a Person on Fire

Sieze a blanket from a bed or any woolen material. Hold the corners and stretch them higher than your head. Rush boldly on the person. The next instant throw the unfortunate person on the floor. Any remnant of flame can be put out more leisurely. The next instant immerse the burnt part in cold water, and all pain will cease with the rapidity of magic. Next get some common flour and cover the burned parts with an inch thickness of flour. Let the flour remain until it falls off itself, when a new skin will be found.

Faith of Our Fathers

The noblest question in the world is,
"What good may I do in it?"

Benjamin Franklin

St. Francis of Assisi Catholic Church

The Catholic Church in Bend dates back to 1904. Father Michael Hickey said the first mass in a hall over the Bend Mercantile Store. The congregation consisted of seven families and five single men. Although Father Hickey was only able to visit once a year, the Catholics continued to gather every Sunday.

In 1909, the Bishop of Baker, Charles O'Reilly, asked the Superiors of the Franciscan Capuchin Fathers of Ireland to send priests to his diocese. Father Thomas Dowling and Father Luke Sheehan arrived in 1910. Father Luke became the first pastor in 1911 when a little church on Bond Street was dedicated in honor of St. Francis of Assisi.

The present church on Lava and Franklin was built in 1920. The altar, a replica of one in Italy, and "Rose windows" were made in Chicago, shipped down the Mississippi and around to The Dalles. Mrs. Cashman donated the pulpit as a memorial to her husband.

The KKK began to harass the Catholics in the early 20s. Once during Mass, the Klan marched in full regalia around the church. They also burned crosses on Pilot Butte. Father Luke asked Mrs. Keller to purchase the Stations of the Cross for the Church when she went to her native Germany. The KKK was rampant when they heard of their delivery. The story went out that, "The Catholics were importing arms and storing them in the basement of the Church." Father Luke arranged for a meeting with the KKK at the old Liberty Theatre. A group of parishioners headed by Jim O'Neill, a 6'5", 250 lb. Irishman, lined the front row seats. Soon thereafter, the incidences ceased.

Mr. and Mrs. Joe Burich donated the first convent for the Sisters at 629 Georgia. The gift of the property was written on a five-cent Christmas card and mailed to Father Luke in 1936 as a Christmas present!

In the midst of the Great Depression Father Luke had E.P. Brosterhous build the first parish-supported Catholic school in the Baker Diocese. The school, at the corner of Bond and Louisiana, opened in September 1936 with 109 students. It closed when a new school was opened in 2000 on 27th Street.

Excerpted from ***St. Francis of Assisi, 1910-1985***

Penny Penhollow and The Lord's Acre

Carroll Penhollow

Some men, it seems, are born for the pulpit and see no reason to quit despite their age. When he was 71, Penny Penhollow was asked by a Bulletin reporter, "When are you retiring?" "Why should I retire?" he replied. "I'll probably die in the pulpit."

My dad, DeVere Lannis Penhollow, better known as Penny, made his entrance into the world in 1907 and preached his first sermon at seventeen. By the time he was 23 he was leading the singing for evangelistic meetings in Redmond and Prineville. The Redmond Christian Church asked him to come and be their minister, but he declined, saying he didn't feel qualified to do that. Instead he enrolled in the Bible Institute of Los Angeles. He stayed in school long enough to feel comfortable calling himself a pastor, though he wasn't able to stay long enough to earn a degree. (Many years later, in 1982, he was given an honorary Doctorate of Divinity from Northwest Christian College in Eugene.)

On his return to Redmond in 1933, Penny Penhollow became the minister of the Redmond Christian Church for a salary of $12.00 a week. When the war broke out, ministers were in short supply in the Central Oregon area and Dad became a modern day circuit rider preaching at Sisters, Powell Butte, Madras and Culver. Sometimes he would give his sermon two or three places on a single Sunday, then return home in the evening in time to milk his cows.

In 1943, Grandma Bussett from Powell Butte, visited Dad and asked him to come to Powell Butte to preach. There wasn't an organized church there but they had a small church building of sorts. It was three small schools they had pulled together over the years to form a single structure. Dad went to Powell Butte and stayed for 46 years.

The church grew rather significantly and it became apparent that they needed a new building. The question was how to pay for it. Being a small farming community, they didn't have the resources to finance a project of that magnitude. In 1947 the members worked out a plan to raise the money. The idea came from a magazine called The Farmers' Federation. An article told how a Black church in South Carolina had entered into a Lord's Acre Program. Each farm family was to dedicate one acre of land to the Lord's Acre project. The proceeds from that acre would be donated to the church.

The first Lord's Acre sale was held in 1947. The auction items included 315 sacks of certified seed potatoes, 300 sacks of commercial potatoes, 1 purebred Guernsey heifer, 2 fat steers, some prime calves, 6 feeder pigs, numerous ducks, a lot of chickens and several geese, tons of grain and some handmade items.

What was to become a famous pit barbecue was also introduced that year. Mr. C.C. Vice said, "I read somewhere in a magazine how to barbecue beef. I'd never tried it before, but we all got together, dug a pit and went at it. And it was never better done." The menu was 1 large bun with meat and barbecue sauce, beans, coffee and a doughnut, topped off with a lip-smacking slice of homemade pie, all for 50 cents! Henry Musick said the beans came out like bullets because they weren't par boiled, but everything else was a hit.

The church grossed $5,968.00. From the beginning, 10 per cent of the proceeds went to missions. The remaining 90 per cent was used for construction and maintenance of the present facility and for bible college support and scholarships.

The Lord's Acre has always taken a lot of preparation. In addition to baked goods and canned goods, the ladies made quilts and other needlework. As soon as one year's sale was finished, they started on the next. The men of the church were responsible for the barbecue. Most times it took a week to prepare the meat, beans and potatoes.

There's never been a failure. Oh, there's been some severe weather situations, but the barbecue and the Lord's Acre have come through.

Over the years the Lord's Acre has attracted people from all across the Northwest, California and even back east. John F. Kennedy was there one year with Jacqueline while he was still a senator campaigning for the Presidency. They purchased a quilt from Mrs. Yates. Hubert Humphrey came too.

Because it's on the first Saturday in November and the huge crowds it attracts, the Lord's Acre has been a favorite place for politicians to shake hands and be seen in their search for votes. Senator Wayne Morse often purchased a truckload of hay. The Smothers Brothers even came one year but they didn't formally entertain.

For many of those who live in this area, the Lord's Acre is synonymous with Powell Butte and Penny Penhollow. We know that as the years pass there will be fewer and fewer people left who remember the preacher who occupied the pulpit when this annual event was started. Yet his spirit lives on in the community and there will always be some who sense his presence around the barbecue pit.

As told to Charlene & David Blahnik

Carroll Penhollow and his brothers Clyde, William, Michael, James and Terry are natives of Central Oregon.

Penny's Favorite Pie
Sour Cream Raisin Pie

1 c. raisins	1/2 tsp. each salt, cinnamon, nutmeg and cloves
1 c. sugar	1 tsp. vinegar
1 egg	1 c. thick sour cream
1 tsp. flour	

Add raisins to unbaked piecrust. Mix sugar, cream, spices & egg & pour over raisins. Bake 45 minutes at 350 degrees.

The Pulpit Pounding Preacher and His Fine Stubborn Son

Rev. A.C. Mize and Roy Mize

"When the goin' gets tough, the tough get goin'," could have been my father and grandfather's philosophy for living.

My dad, Roy Mize, moved our family to Bend from Brush, Colorado in 1936 after Grandpa, the Reverend A.C. Mize, wrote to him saying, "Come, you'll find work here."

Finding work wasn't as easy. Every day he showed up at the Shevlin-Hixon mill and joined the line of men looking for a job. After hearing "No work today, boys," most of the disappointed men went home, but Dad stayed and positioned himself where the superintendent had to walk by him. He called the boss by name and asked, "You got any work today?" Finally the superintendent gave him a job because this stubborn man wouldn't go home after being told "no."

Roy Mize was a good provider. When other families were hungry and couldn't pay the electric bill, our stomachs were full. There was plenty of venison and rainbow trout on the table.

Dad also went out into the woods to cut firewood. Most folks cooked on a wood stove. He used to tell a story about a friend who went wood cutting. When the pickup was loaded with rounds, he headed home stopping at a gas station. He met with his friend, Kenny Roach, the game warden. They leaned against the load on the back of the truck and talked a while. When he finally crawled back into the driver's seat to go home, Kenny beckoned to him and said, "One more thing before you go. I'd advise you to get that load of wood home before it bleeds to death."

The man thanked him and drove home to unload the wood and the illegal buck deer he'd shot and stashed under his load of wood. For years I thought that hunter-woodsman was my dad because we always had venison on the table. It was so like him that I was disappointed when my brother Larry told me it wasn't really him.

Preaching was the way of life for my grandpa, A.C. Mize, who had come to Bend in 1935 to reorganize the Nazarene Church. The church was so affected by the Depression there were only nine members and a Sunday School enrollment of thirty-five. Hardship and small numbers didn't scare him though. He was what's known as a church planter. He'd go into an area, build a building and establish a congregation. He'd preach until a full time preacher was sent. Once the new preacher was settled, Grandpa moved on to plant another church.

Grandpa could preach! He was a hell-fire and brimstone preacher. Many a man and woman accepted Jesus as Lord of their lives from the fear of going to the hell that Grandpa so vividly described. Grandpa was a pulpit-pounder and I remember his booming voice telling me I should never smoke cigarettes, drink alcohol, wear jewelry or makeup, attend movies or dances or do so many of the other things that seemed like such fun to my young, curious mind. I also remember being determined to try them all once I grew up and got on my own!

Most of all I remember Grandpa Mize as a praying man; a generous, holy, caring man whose congregation loved him dearly. I look back now and realize it was a healthy and proper fear of God he instilled in me and I consider that a timeless gift from the only grandpa I ever knew.

By Barbara Mize Baumgardner

Alfred Courtright Mize, 1871-1947, came to Bend in 1935 to pastor the Nazarene Church. One of his seven children, LeRoy Mize, 1909 - 1990, followed him to Bend in 1936. He owned Mize Plumbing and Heating Co. and did the early plumbing work at Mt. Bachelor.

Century to Century: Fulfilling the Vision

By Judy Osgood

Historical records don't tell us where Rev. B. Harper preached his first sermon in Bend, or what he was wearing, but we know that it was around 1900. People must have listened because he then went on to establish the First Presbyterian Church in 1903 under the sponsorship of the Presbyterian Board of Missions. A little log schoolhouse located in what is now Drake Park served as the site.

As attendance grew, the congregation's need for a permanent home became evident and in 1913 they built and dedicated a facility on Franklin Street that is now considered an important historical landmark. That facility with its beautiful stained glass windows, currently houses the Spiritual Awareness Center.

The Presbyterians outgrew that building too, but they didn't have the capital to fund a new facility. Years later Leo Bishop reported that when the land became available, the church had about $200 cash and it was in a cigar box that the church secretary kept under her bed for safekeeping. Lack of cash wasn't a deterrent for that faith-filled congregation; it was just a hurdle to get over.

The land they wanted was the 7-acre site across from the current Bend High School football field. As they had less than a week to raise the money to buy the property, a group of women led by Florence Marshall, Evelyn Graham and Alice Bishop called every member of the church asking for pledges. When the calling was done they were still short, so they went back and called everybody again asking them to dig deeper and this time, when the calls were completed, they had the money they needed. Then they had to finance a new building. That facility was completed in 1962 when Rev. Jim McGuigin was pastor and it was expanded in the early 1980s.

And still they grew. "Century to Century, Fulfilling the Vision" was the theme for the fundraising campaign for the new sanctuary that was completed in February of 1998. Why that theme? Because it was the congregation's desire to build a spiritual home for Presbyterians and friends of the congregation in the 21st century, as those men and women who gathered in the little log schoolhouse in the park at the beginning of the 20th century had done for them.

Women Who Dared

Never say die.
Be stubborn. Be persistent.
Anything worth having is worth
striving for with all your might.

Orville Redenbacher, Popcorn Magnate

Les Schwab's Paper Stars

Barbara Mize Baumgardner

Most folks around Central Oregon associate Les Schwab with the tire business. After all, his name was displayed on 300 tire stores in the Northwest by 2001. However, back in the 40s, long before he was worrying about treads and rubber statistics, he was the circulation manager for The Bend Bulletin.

At 14, I was the first girl paper carrier in Bend and it was Les Schwab who doled out the 135 newspapers I delivered on my route six days a week. In his book, **Les Schwab: Pride in Performance**, he talks about getting discouraged with some of his paper boys not doing the job they'd been hired for. So one day he decided to try girl paper carriers and found out that it worked well. He called me his "star paper girl" because I got less complaints and more new customers than the boys did, and I frequently won the $25.00 savings bond prize that was given to one carrier each month for good performance.

While writing this story I learned that Rosie Rosengarth Gustafson also made the claim to being Schwab's first paper girl. In fact, her sister told me "she'd fight me for the title." To settle it Rosie and I dug out the old boxes of stored stuff from when we were kids and we both came up with newspaper clippings to prove our claims. After checking the dates, we found I truly was the first, but not the only. She became a paper carrier two years after me and she, too, won a $20.00 prize for being an honor carrier.

I thought the issue was settled until I got a note in the mail from her telling me there was another young entrepreneur who also won the exact same award. Rosie said, "She needs to be mentioned because she - whoever she was - was also considered the "First Girl Ever." And all three of us, of course, were Les Schwab stars.

One hundred thirty five newspapers was a big load on my girl's bicycle and eventually it caused my bike to snap at the lower curve. My dad welded it back together and also welded a bar holding the front frame to the back so it wouldn't break again from the weight of the paper bag.

One of the carriers, Joe Dysart, teased me unmercifully about being such a fat girl that I broke my bicycle. Mr. Schwab tried to support me through Joe's teasing, but he couldn't get Joe to let up. "Someday you'll have to put him in his place," he told me, but he didn't tell me how to do it. One day in the alley behind The Bulletin I "decked" Joe Dysart. He never saw it coming and I didn't give it any forethought. I just doubled up my fist and came from down low, catching Joe under the chin with enough force to put him down flat on the blacktop. Pretty good swing for a girl! Joe never said a word and neither did Mr. Schwab. He just gave me that "Atta Girl" look and went about helping us kids get our papers ready for delivery.

Funny how it changed the way Joe treated me. I never got teased after that. In fact all the guys seemed to find a new respect for me that they didn't have before, and Mr. Schwab seemed a little prouder of his "star paper girl."

Barbara (Mize) Baumgardner, b. 1931 in Colorado, moved to Central Oregon in 1936. She traveled in Europe and the U.S. after being widowed in 1981. She is a freelance writer, having authored 3 books and numerous articles.

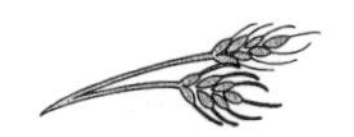

Craig and Lola on Badger

The Reserve Champion's Doll

Lola Owen

Idaho may be known as the Potato State, but those wonderful, edible tubers have played a big role in Central Oregon too. I know because my family raised them.

Next to the lumber industry, they were the biggest source of income in Redmond when I was growing up. During the harvest all the neighbors would come and help you, and you'd help everybody else. You'd go from one farm to the next. My mother would make great big huge dinners for the harvesting crew; homemade pies and chicken and gravy and potatoes. The Indians also came from Warm Springs to help bring in the crop. They especially liked our farm because the biggest juniper tree in the area was on it. That's where they used to have their pow-wows.

Potatoes were a source of good times for us too, in addition to being our livelihood. We had a Potato Festival with princesses from the different schools and a Potato Queen, and dancing and bands and a parade. The farmers brought in their different potatoes to be judged as the champion ones for their area.

Our other big event of the year was the fair. Lots of children were involved in the 4-H shows and judging. The most fun I had was when I beat the boys in showmanship. First I won the dairy showmanship award, then the all-around showmanship where you had to show a pig, a sheep, a dairy animal and a beef animal. For the two years following that I won the grand championship and finally, the next two years I was reserve champion. I still have all those ribbons as well as all those wonderful memories.

I met my future husband, Curt, at work but I had to ask him for our first date. He was a little older than I was and he was afraid to ask me out. We went to the drive-in and the Spring Frolic. That was the big dance where all the counties - Deschutes, Crook and Jefferson got together. It was a big fling and lots of fun.

My husband and I met in January and got married the next December 30th, 1955. Up 'til then I'd gotten a doll for Christmas every single year. When nobody gave me one that year, I wailed about the fact I didn't get my doll. Whether she had it for me all along or not, I don't know, but when my great aunt came down the reception line she handed me a special gift to open, and it was a doll in a crocheted wedding dress.

As told to Lorna Cerenzia

Lola Eby Owen, b. 1936 is a native of Redmond, Oregon. Her grandparents, Ezra and Lottie Eby were the second homesteaders in the Redmond area. They founded the Presbyterian Church in Redmond, Nov. 25th, 1906

Kathleen Lenore Bacon

When World War II started it seemed like all the young men left to enlist. My brother Bob went into the airforce, I went into the fields to help my parents and Granddad Skelton get our crops in. We had to do it ourselves. My Dad made a pick-up baler. We pulled the baler along with a tractor. He built a platform to stand on so he could feed the hay into the baler. The bales were left behind the machine just as they are today. I drove the tractor, Mother pushed wires through the block holes, Granddad tied the wires, and Daddy fed the machine. Because I had a terrible time turning the equipment around at the end of the rows, Dad motioned which way I was to turn the wheels on the tractor to back the baler around and get started down the row again. No wonder Dad lost all his hair; I bet he wondered how he could have such a dumb daughter!

Bill Thomas Ranch 1920

Born to Ride

Barbara Meyers

I was born in McMinnville to Bill and Loma Thomas but moved to Central Oregon when my father inherited land there after World War I. He was a real cowboy and mother was a school teacher. The house I lived in until I was 13 was a god-forsaken rundown place. We had 16 horses, 4 sows, cows and a thousand white-legged chickens. As a child I lived to ride.

My pony's name was Babe and I started riding her when I was 4 years old. I would ride her all over the ranch. One day I asked my mother to saddle her but she said no because she was napping. Not to be denied, I went out and put the saddle on myself. But since I was so small I did not get the cinch very tight. As we galloped across the fields the saddle slid under her stomach and I was caught in the stirrup. Babe drug me - I don't know how far - but instead of running and jumping she just slowly walked along. I was lucky that she loved me so much.

We had some calves and I used to go out in the pen and I'd ride 'em. My dad would always say, "Don't do that, they're going to buck you off." One day when he was in the fields I conveniently forgot what he told me, and got on a calf. Just as my dad predicted, he bucked me off - into a fresh manure pile with my face down! Well, that was the end of my riding the calves.

When I was about 6 years old we went to a circus in Madras. There I saw beautiful girls ride two horses, with a foot on each one. I thought that was great and got really excited about it. When I got home I got my pony and my dad's pony, put them next to each other and stood up with a foot on each back. Like those girls in the circus I was ready to go but they took off in opposite directions and I darn near broke my neck.

When I was about seven and it was time for me to go to school, I had to move away from the ranch. The first year I lived in a boarding house in Madras but the next year my mother moved to Madras and my brother and I lived with her in a one-room place so we could get an education.

In 1936 I started high school in Madras. It was a lovely school and I really liked going to it. When it burned down after my second year there, our classes were held in the basement of an old hotel and the Madras community hall was used as our high school gym.

I graduated as valedictorian in 1940. Although I edited the school paper throughout high school, and was Jefferson County's first 4-H outstanding girl, it was the honor of being Jefferson County's first rodeo queen that was foreshadowed by those early days on the ranch and my fascination with the animals I could ride.

As told to Rosa Lewis

Barbara Jeanne (Thomas) Meyers was born in McMinnville, OR, in 1921. She moved to Madras in 1929 and has lived in Sisters and Redmond. She has had an active career and served as a leader in many community organizations as well as raising six children.

Rural Photojournalist
Martha Stranahan

Our oldest son was born on January 2, 1943. My husband was in Africa and Rommel was chasing his outfit across Tunisia. The Rose Bowl had been moved to the East Coast because of the Japanese threat at Pearl Harbor. I listened to the game on the radio. That year Oregon State College played Duke University.

After the Second World War was over my husband had back pay coming, as he had been a prisoner of war in Germany. We had not seen the western United States so we loaded our old Ford and took off for California staying in motels along the way, such as they were. Very often they were just rented rooms in homes scattered across the country.

We lived in California six months with some of my husband's relatives. In 1946 we headed for Washington intending to live there, but along the way we stopped in Bend, really liked it, and stayed. At the time I was about 30 years old.

I worked for forty years as a photojournalist in Central Oregon and I had some interesting experiences. Once I was taken in a helicopter with Earl Thompson. He was a spotter and an observer for Bonneville Power

Administration looking after their high voltage lines which went along the Deschutes River crossing the Columbia River at The Dalles or Hood River. That made an interesting story for Central Electric Cooperative which was my writing source along with the Central Oregon Rancher and the Redmond Spokesman.

Most of the time I traveled in my own car to ranches, farms, rural businesses and families in the area who were served by the Co-op, which was headquartered in Redmond. I covered a lot of cattle ranches. The owners would take me out in their pickups to show me their places, but I never could get in and out of those vehicles easily. They were too steep and too far up and down for me. Long ago I lost count of the fences I climbed over and under, but it was a lot. During those years I saw the development of various breeds of cattle and lots of horses. Some of the stories I wrote were about families with notable horses that they raced or bred to sell their offspring.

One of the most interesting places I visited was Fred Hodecker's potato cellar in Madras. It had been an abandoned strip of railroad, like a spur line or a siding, and he converted it to a cellar that provided a dry, warm constant temperature to store his crop.

Other people have made the big journeys. They've been in foreign lands while I've stayed close to home. What they've done, the places they've gone to, the people they've met and interviewed are really interesting and fun to read about, but that wasn't for me. My adventures have been vicarious ones through the people I've interviewed close to home. Their stories are important too, and writing them has been very satisfying. To the extent that I've brought them to life for my readers, I've met my goals and been successful. This land is my land, and it's where I was meant to be.

As told to Lorna Cerenzia

Martha Stranahan, 1916-2002. She graduated from Westminster College in New Wilmington, PA. She moved to Bend in 1946. Martha wrote extensively about the people and life in Central Oregon.

Destined, Determined and Eager to Fly

Maggie Sink

Maggie Sink was an early day aviatrix who, like her husband, and her brother Guy Welch, was among Redmond Airport's pioneer movers and shakers.

Although initially leery of flying, she felt destined to take to the skies. She met her future husband in California and he took her for a spin that scared her, but didn't change her mind about wanting to be a pilot herself. Three weeks after meeting they were married.

Red taught Maggie to fly in eight different planes, but she preferred biplanes so she could put her head out and look over the scenery. When he was teaching her to fly he would only let her make approaches and then land at the end of her lesson because they had to save the landing gear for the paying students.

The Sinks were true barnstormers of the 1930s. With low horsepower planes they traveled Arizona, California and Oregon teaching people to fly, helping to establish new airfields and revitalizing the neglected ones.

The summer of 1940 found the pair operating the Roseburg airport and frequently hopping over the Cascades to instruct Redmond residents at the old American Legion airstrip that was located half a mile east of the present flight service station.

On one visit, the Sinks met J.R. Roberts who was an early aviation enthusiast and civic leader. He urged them to move their flight operations to Redmond. Prompted by the invitation and good weather, they built a three-plane hangar and office.

Volunteers stretched a 1,700-foot landing strip through the gnarled junipers. Across the hangar front they hung the sign “Roberts Field” proclaiming that Redmond had joined the nation’s aviation community. Maggie’s brother Guy was the airstrip/weather station manager from August 1941 until the army started construction on the air base.

Before December 7, 1941, many local residents earned their wings at the new airport under the Civilian Pilot Training Program, the government’s effort to create a pool of pre-trained pilots in the event the United States was drawn into the European conflict.

War did come. Red Sink and Guy Welch joined the Army Air Corps and Maggie closed the hangar doors for the last time. The Army Corps of Engineers moved into the field and it became the huge complex of a bomber base.

Following railroads and pavement, Maggie flew to Texas and joined the new Women’s Auxiliary Service Pilots (WASP) of Sweetwater. It was one of the first groups of women pilots to ferry military aircraft from factory to training fields.

Maj. Sink was in war service all over Europe and the Pacific. After WW II, he bought an airport near Vallejo, California but in less than a year he was called back to active service. While landing in Mobile, a plane cut across his runway killing him and leaving Maggie to run their new airport on her own.

Excerpted from an interview by Martha Stranahan
for The Redmond Spokesman

A Hiker For All Seasons

Myrtice Morrison

Her love affair with the woods began during her childhood in Gates, Oregon. Myrtice's father took her and her siblings hiking all the time when they were growing up. Both of her parents were botanists and from them she learned to identify the trees and plants and flowers. When she grew up she married a forester and he was eventually transferred to Bend.

When friends here said they wished they had somebody to go walking with, she jumped up and volunteered to lead hikes. "I just wanted to be outside," she said. That was in 1979 and she still goes twice a week, although last year she turned the leadership for longer hikes over to one of the men with a GPS.

For the first 12 years of her "official hiking career," she worked for Bend Metro Parks and Recreation, and since then has led hikes on her own and through the Bend Senior Center. When she started, her husband was bedridden because of a series of strokes and going meant that she had to get somebody to take care of him. The time away from that responsibility, the joy of being outdoors and the physical exercise provided a welcomed and healthy change of pace for her. And the company was fun. There were usually at least 10 to 12 hikers in the group, depending on the weather. The group that met on Mondays hiked up to 5 miles while the group that hiked on Thursdays went 5 to 10.

Since she is very comfortable using a compass, she never hesitated to take the hikers places she had never been to before. "I was brought up in the forest living out in remote places," she said, "and I was never afraid. Out west of here on the trails there'd be fresh bear tracks and bear sign. Logs would be freshly torn up where they had hunted for ants, so we were really cautious when we saw that. Usually the trails were good. We never got lost but we did get turned around a few times."

Crossing log bridges was tricky, but only once in all those years has one of her hikers gone into the water enough to get really wet. "We used walking sticks and were mighty cautious," she said. If they didn't have a railing on each side of the log, they used walking sticks that were long enough to reach down to the creek bed. "There would be a few slips and falls on the trail but we'd get up and go on. People just took it in their stride. They didn't get mad because the hike was too rough. If someone felt it was too tough and didn't feel like going any further, they'd stay by the trailside until we came back for them.

Sometimes in the winter when there is snow on the ground here, or in the spring when the wildflowers are in bloom, we choose to do desert hikes and go as far east as Fort Rock. Even the early spring flowers are different there than the early spring flowers in the mountains." They go south as far as La Pine, southwest to the McKenzie Pass area, and northeast to the Ochocos. There are some special places they return to every year but in addition she said, "I always like to find places that the average tourist and local resident doesn't know about."

When she talks about her hiking experiences it is hard to separate what Myrtice has done in the past from what she is doing now. She is still leading hikes almost a quarter of a century after she hopped up and volunteered to lead the first one. They are still going up to 6 to 10 miles on Mondays and Thursdays and anyone who contacts Juniper Park can still find out how to join her.

As told to Carol Swift

Myrtice Morrison, was born in 1920 in Hazel Green (near Salem), Oregon and moved to Bend in 1978. She graduated from Oregon State University where she met her husband Fritz. His career was in forestry and they moved throughout the northwest working on projects such as Bonneville and the Coulee Dam. She often helped by cooking for the bachelors working on the projects.

A Pioneer Spirit Lives on in Redmond

Darleen Dillon

Redmond was a different place when my husband, Jack Dillon, and I moved there in1955. He had an auto body shop where the Plum Fierce filling station is now. I worked too and rode my horse back and forth from our home near Cinder Butte. There wasn't much traffic and the cars that were on the road respected horses, not honking at them.

You could walk through Redmond and say hello to everyone. I used to love it when the cowboys came to town and told their tales about Prineville, which wasn't as gentle and tame as Redmond. At that time they were still shooting sheepherders.

I always wanted my own horse, so after I was married I started saving my pennies. When they finally totaled three dollars, I bought my first one in 1944. From then on it was trading and trading. After I trained that first horse to work I sold him and eventually I was able to upgrade to the point where I had an Arabian stallion and several mares. We had Arabians for awhile. Then I started raising Tennessee Walkers.

When I was a young teenager I started making my own clothes and from childhood on I always had a big garden. Although we have a few sheep, I no longer shear them myself, but I still spin the fleece into yarn and weave it into fabric or knit or crochet clothing. I buy wheat from Culver Seed Growers and grind my own flour. You don't know what good is unless you've had bread made from fresh ground flour!

As told to Lorna Cerenzia

Darleen Dillon, born in 1923 in Princeton, Nebraska, moved to Redmond in 1955. She worked as a farmer's wife but has enjoyed riding many mountain trails on horseback and making crafts.

Zucchini Patties

3 c. shredded zucchini
1 1/4 c. biscuit mix
1 c. grated cheddar cheese
2 eggs
onion
salt

Mix well and fry as patties.

Recipe from Darlene Dillon.

Fay Young, Wayne Jacobs, Marvin Jacobs, Wesley Tittle, Vernon Luff

Milking Cows, Picking Rocks, and Moving Pipe

Bev Clarno

It must have been in 1942 when I moved here. My parents had separated so we moved in with my uncle, Fay Young, who had a dairy outside of Redmond, near Cinder Butte. It was the first time I'd been on a farm, but I learned how to milk cows and do my share of the chores. We'd get up at 3:30 in the morning, help milk those 200 cows, go to school, then come home at 3:30 in the afternoon and milk cows again.

In September they let school out for picking potatoes and everybody had to help with that too. They had a belt you put on your waist with hooks in it and a gunnysack. I suppose they weighed about seventy pounds when they were full. That's a lot of weight, especially when you're bent over all day dragging it behind you as it filled. For every sack of potatoes you filled up they gave you six cents, and that's the way I always made my money for my school clothes.

Eventually my mom got her own rental. Us kids had to stay alone out back of the house we rented because Mom worked at the market and would only allow us to go in there once a day. I was about ten and we really didn't have any toys. However, some guy who worked with Mom made us stilts and I went everywhere on them. And I was really good! They probably weren't very high but they sure seemed that way to me.

Another man showed us how to take tin cans and mash ‘em to fit your foot so you could walk on them and that was fun too.

During high school it was my brother’s job and mine to farm with a team of horses. First we hooked them up to what was called a stone boat, which is a long wooden sled that is low to the ground and has runners on it. Then our job was to load rocks from the fields onto it, get them out of the fields and pile them on the rock wall fences that had been started. Every time we plowed it, we’d plow up more rocks. It was just a typical farm with turkeys, chickens, rabbits and five cows, which I milked before and after school. And, of course, we put up all our own food. There wasn’t any indoor plumbing for us. We had an outhouse and took a bath on the kitchen floor in a tin tub on Saturdays. You heated water on the wood stove and then poured it in the tin tub, put some chairs around the tub and draped some towels around the chairs in case anyone came in the kitchen. But it still wasn’t very private.

Where we farmed was close to the Crooked River at the Smith Rocks. We had a flat down below. My brother and I had to go down there to change the irrigation pipes in the evening and the next morning, so my stepfather would say, “There’s no use you coming home, you take your dinners and something for breakfast and spend the night.” So, Mom would wrap us something to eat in cloth napkins and we’d take our sleeping bags and spend the night. There were a lot of rattlesnakes and I was terrified of them, but my brother would hunt them down and kill ‘em. He had a whole shoe box full of those rattlers.

I was also afraid of our hay chopper, which was a big, noisy thing. Whatever went down inside of it would be chopped up, like your body or anything. Once a pitchfork got away from me and it was chopped up so fine that the metal pitch fork tines came out about an inch long.

In some of the fields we didn’t have pipes so we used flood irrigating. You’d open the head gates and water would come down the ditch so you could flood the field. First, you’d go lay down a piece of canvas on a rod in the ditch and make a seal all around it with a shovel of mud so that when the water hits it, it dams it up and the water goes out into the fields. My brother and I would let the water go first and race down to the canvas dam because we didn’t want to have to go clear back to the gate. Sometimes we made it and sometimes we had to race back and shut the water off again. And then it was even harder because the dirt was all mud and wouldn't work well.

But the thing I remember most was, even though we all worked very hard, my uncle made sure everybody got to go to the dances. Uncle had a country western band called The Crooked River Ramblers. He played the accordion, was self taught and, oh my, he was good. A lot of farmers played in that band. During the war they'd play at the hall, which was at the airbase outside of Redmond, and at all the Grange halls too.

I'd go as a little kid and listen to the music. Then I learned square dancing and country dancing at an early age. Many of the adults had their drinks, including home brew, in the courtyard in their cars. Outside, not inside the Grange hall. That was mostly the men. A few women would drink but mostly just the guys would go outside and talk. And then the women would have to go outside and drag 'em back in if they wanted to dance.

You danced until you got tired and then you sat on the benches and chairs along the edge of the hall. The ladies brought in pies and cakes and a snack at eleven o'clock at night. After that we'd dance some more. A lot of the women would wear out, so these old men would grab me to dance. And man, I just loved it. I always liked to dance.

That was the way of life, to go do something at the Grange hall. Families did things together back then. It was a good life, and all that hard work was great preparation for the things I did as an adult, including the time I spent in the state legislature.

As told to Ray Miao

Bev Clarno was born in Langlois, Oregon in 1936 and moved to Central Oregon in 1942. She worked as a Circuit Court clerk in Bend. She served as a state legislator where she was the second woman to serve as the Speaker of the House and is currently a State Senator. Bev is also a private pilot.

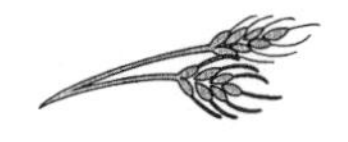

THE BEND BULLETIN, BEND, ORE., WEDNESDAY, AUGUST 30, 1933

For the LOVE of EVE by Lucy Walling

BEGIN HERE TODAY

Eve Bayless, pretty assistant to Earle Barnes, advertising manager of Bixby's department store, marries Dick Judey, a construction superintendent temporarily working in Lake City. Dick wants Eve to give up working but she refuses.

Arlene Smith, stenographer in the advertising office, fancies herself in love with George Bliss, but he is vamped by Mona Allen, trouble-making copy writer.

Eve receives a letter from Irene Prentiss, former schoolmate who is playing the stock market. Eve decides to do the same thing. Without Dick's knowledge she borrows money from her mother and buys stock.

...

the dressing room elevator and she saw modern conveniences in almost luxurious form for the comfort of the actors and actresses. She was particularly impressed with the laundry and drying room and the nursery for the children of the stage-folk. Eve looked down at the stage from the fly-loft and became slightly dizzy.

...ped into the elevator again. They descended to a room opposite the wings, beautifully decorated in white and gold. In the center was a billiard table, and great, soft easy chairs were grouped about. "No matter what its color scheme may ... room is called the green ... Dick explained. ...

... Snatches of melo... Dick glanced ... Eve close in the ... for a brief in...

... the new stage."

...

"Don't be so gullible ... girl is no saint."

Marya ... window, merely looked up at them and smiled. What Marya thought, no one knew.

When Mona returned to her desk she did not glance at either of the other girls. Her features were without expression as she folded a few sheets of fresh copy paper, picked up a pencil and left the office.

"She's probably gone to see George Bliss on the pretense of asking what's new in the fur department," commented Arlene. "Well, I've got plenty of work to do myself and I must say I can do it a lot better when Mona is far, far away." Arlene began to type rapidly.

* * *

Eve was tempted to tell Dick about the luncheon with Theron Reece and explain how it had come about but she decided that to do so would be to attach importance to the incident. It did not occur to her to discuss her venture on the stock market with Dick. In that matter she wished to play a lone hand until she had achieved results.

Hence she encouraged him to talk about his work.

"I'll take you out to see the theater Sunday morning," he told her. "It's going to be ready for the public in two weeks. Just now the auditorium is being decorated and ...

... more than that to ... feeling she had ... past week seemed ... her. Dick was all ... consideration and Eve ... of the fact that she ... him, even for a moment ... resolved to make this up ... the future. Dick's love was the most important thing ... world for her and she wanted ... know it.

... curled up in a lounge chair that afternoon with a new book. She made it a point to bring home a book from the circulating library each week-end. After she finished reading the book Eve always entered its title and the name of its author in a tiny notebook she carried in her purse. She had begun this system when she was in high school and had followed it faithfully ever since.

* * *

Monday morning Eve returned to her work as though inspired. She thought of the actresses soon to come to Lake City for the opening of the theater and decided to make an especial bid for their patronage in the store advertising she wrote. Barnes commended her for her foresight.

That noon Eve accompanied Marya to a Scottish tearoom where a twinkling-eyed Highland lassie told their fortunes by reading the leaves in their teacups. Eve attached no significance to the prophecies made for her but Marya was apparently overjoyed because the seeress predicted she would soon be married. Eve smiled to herself. It would not take a fortune teller to predict marriage for a girl so sweet and lovely as Marya.

* * *

When the home edition of the evening newspaper was delivered to the office Eve turned to the financial pages. Strange, she thought, how light-hearted she had been but an hour before and now her world was plunged into gloom. Pure Soap, Inc. had gone down a point ...

...

On Sunday morning, as he had promised, Dick tucked Eve into the roadster and drove the short distance to the new building. The white brick and terra cotta structure loomed ...

...

The Bend chamber of commerce, by the president, Walter G. Coombs, headed the list of six signing the blanket NRA code today. This brings the list of those to whom the blue ...

Men Who Made a Difference

The people we admire in our lives are ordinary people who have been able to accomplish some extraordinary things. The things that make them extraordinary are things that we all possess.

Rolf Bernirschke, 1983 NFL Man of the Year

Les Schwab and son with Evans Fly Company Softball Team

The Tough Years
Les Schwab

Although I was born here in Bend, my parents moved back to Minnesota when I was a year and a half old and didn't return to the area until I was 12. That was in 1929, right in the middle of the Depression and it was pretty tough going. My mother died when I was a sophomore, and that fall our dad died too, leaving my brother and me on our own. I'm proud to say that neither of us ever took one dollars worth of relief money. We made our own way and paid for our own keep at a boarding house in Bend that specialized in high school kids whose families lived out of town.

I had a paper route for the old Oregon Journal. That first route only had about thirty customers on it, but I guess I was a hustler and impressed my boss with my willingness to work hard. When I told him I was planning to go to Washington State to live with an aunt and uncle, he said, "You stay here. I'll fire the boy that has the downtown route and you can have the newsstands and keep your old route too." With that arrangement I made $35 a month. I paid $15 a month room and board, so that was $20 I could spend and that was great.

At the beginning I delivered all the papers on a bicycle. When we started a motor route the next year out there on Arnold Market Road, I bought an old car, but I had enough sense not to use it except for delivering the Sunday paper. So that'd be another $30 a month I made. And then, between my junior and senior year, he gave me the whole town. I made more money than the high school principal.

The Journal was a morning paper. It came on the train at about a quarter to eight. I had to make arrangements with the school for being late. I remember, they always gave me study hall the first period, and I'd pick up my work at school when I got there. So, I didn't do very good in school but I did pretty good in business.

The newspapers in those days were fighting for circulation. The Oregon Journal and the Oregonian were pretty close, and I hustled pretty good for the Oregon Journal. I guess that's why they gave me all those routes. After I graduated from high school, I went to work for the Oregon Journal full time.

Eventually I became a district manager. The territory covered most of Eastern Oregon up to Yakima, Washington. I'd drive all over the state to get delivery boys and help them out and try to give them some idea about how to do a little more business and make some money. The boys were seventh and eighth graders. We'd have contests and give away bicycles and stuff. They liked that. I'd usually tell the young people, "This is your first job. I want you to be successful."

When I started my tire stores, our average store size was about five to ten employees. I told my store mangers the same thing. I'd say, "If you have ten employees, you see to it that you have ten successful employees. You make them successful, what happens to you? You're successful. What happens if you have ten failures? Well, you're an ex-store manager."

It's pretty simple business philosophy, but it works. And it all started way back with the boys delivering newspapers, back when times were really tough.

As told by Ray Miao

Les Schwab was born in Bend in 1917. He bought the OK Rubber Welders shop in Prineville and turned that into Les Schwab Tires with headquarters in Prineville. It is now the second largest chain of independent tire stores in the country.

Making Your Own Luck

Vern Patrick

I came to Redmond in 1948 and operated a pharmacy up into the 90s. During this time I had a chance to visit with a lot of people. We had 2200 people in town at that time. It was a case of everybody knew everybody. You never locked your house and you never took the keys out of your car. It just wasn't necessary.

I had a partner that traveled Washington, Oregon, Northern California and Idaho that financed me. After we set up here, we opened a store at Lebanon. We had two stores in Lebanon at one time. One at Albany. One at Springfield, one in Eugene, one in McMinnville, Cedar Hills, which we still have an interest in and one clear up at Forks, Washington which was the end of the earth at that time.

When we first started out we opened at 7:30 in the morning and closed at 10:00 o'clock at night, six days a week. On Sunday we were open between 9:00 and 12:00 and again from 4:00 to 7:00. So we had four hours a week we could do just anything you wanted to do. The original store here had a wagon wheel red false front. And during one of those four-hour periods I decided to repaint the thing. So I got up on top and I leaned out and the false front leaned right out with me. So I crawled back down. I had painters come and paint the place.

We built the first heated pool in town at our house in 59. Some of those cold mornings the teams would come out and practice in ours. We had lots of kids. One time we went out and counted 104 youngsters in our pool. When we had all those kids in the pool and I was working long hours Madeline, my wife, would do her ironing and whatever else right next to the pool so she could keep an eye on things. We insisted that the kids bring a note before they could swim. Some of the parents apparently couldn't write any better than the kids because we had some strange notes given to us. We rigged up a system of flags. A green flag meant it was open to anybody, yellow was adults only and red meant closed.

Of course, being a volunteer was a very important part of life in Redmond. I joined Kiwanis in about 1952 and the Redmond Volunteer Fire Department in about 1951. I spent better than 15 years in the Fire Department and I'm still a member of Kiwanis and also the Chairman of their Kiwanis Foundation. We've raised over $200,000 to help build the swimming pool. We raised $60,000 to build the stadium that was named Don Rich who happened to be the Athletic Director of Redmond High School and also a member of our club. We sold the seats in the center section for $250 each. Then we took the seat back out to my garage and inscribed the name of the person on it with an indentation type thing. And it's there forever. After that was over with we raised enough money to build two more sections on the Don Rich Stadium. And in so doing we raised a little over $100,000 and we can seat 1,500 people. And there's not a single tax dollar in it. We just approved $10,000 to help the High School build a track. We've built batting cages at the High School, tennis courts and a lot of school related stuff.

I was in the Fire Department with John Berning. He paved the streets in Redmond. He happened to be in the store when the fire whistle blew. He was an older fella and quite large. So we took off for the fire hall and running like mad. And I thought 'Come on John, get outa the way.' And you know, I couldn't catch him. I just couldn't believe that the old guy could run as fast as he did. And I congratulated him and he said, "I'm only good for one block." We've had a lot of fun in the Fire Department. Good bunch of guys. Used to play some tricks on 'em that if you did now, they'd lock you up probably.

Back in 1952 our stores began giving scholarships, a small one, I think $200 or $250 and gradually increased that as time went by. In 1991, Madeline and I set a small amount aside and have been putting into it ever since. We gave our first scholarship in 92. And this year the Cent Wise and we each donated $1,000. And we have enough in the Patrick scholarship that none of the principle is passed out. Only the interest and so this should continue to exist long after we're gone.

I've been very fortunate. They named the elementary school after me. That's one of the greatest honors I've ever had. I think it's because I hired students almost since we've opened the doors. And having the scholarship program and being involved with the Fire Department and all the other things. I don't know, I guess I'm just lucky.

As told to Lorna Cerenzia

Vernon G. Patrick, b. 1922 in Oxford, Nebraska. He attended Idaho State University and was a pharmacist in Redmond for 44 years. He has four sons.

Respected Editor

The Bend Bulletin became a daily newspaper in 1916. George Palmer Putnam and Robert Sawyer were the first two editors/publishers. And then in 1953 Robert W. Chandler, a journalism student at Stanford University, bought The Bulletin and became its third editor.

Bob was born in Marysville, CA. in 1921. He began his career on weekly newspapers in California. He was on the news staff of the San Francisco Chronicle, United Press and The Denver Post before entering Stanford. He served as the editor of the Stanford Review magazine.

Over the next 43 years, Bob grew both the circulation of The Bulletin and his reputation as a tough editor. Bob Welch was one of the many green reporters who worked for Chandler. “Going to work for Bob Chandler fresh out of college was like going to boot camp right out of high school,” he recalls. “He was demanding, uncompromising, a stickler for detail. He was intensely loyal to Central Oregon in general and Bend in particular.”

Welch recounts the legendary dictionary story. “One day, he nailed me on the spelling of a word, which he was forever doing, but I was sure I’d spelled it right. I looked it up in my dictionary. I was right. He was wrong.

I marched into his office, plopped the dictionary down and said, ‘Uh, Mr. Chandler, I spelled the word right.’ He looked at the dictionary, then looked back at me and paused. ‘Welch,’ he said, ‘get a new dictionary.’

Bob Moody, another Bulletin alumnus, said, “I am still asked once in a while, mainly while I am visiting in Bend, if I still work for ‘that S.O.B.’ I’m sure they mean ‘Sweet Old Bob.’ I’ve always been happy to say ‘yes’.”

Chandler was an avid fly fisherman, reader and photographer. But most of all, he loved to fly. Bob was a commercially rated pilot with over 8,500 hours flying time. He flew for business and pleasure to such places as British Columbia, Mexico and El Salvador.

He had a strong interest in higher education and worked to pass the first bill to fund parts of the community college system. Norma Paulus, then Oregon Superintendent of Schools stated, “He was the most powerful voice Central and Eastern Oregon ever had. More, he was just such a major player in state politics and state government decisions. He was an expert in the education system at all levels."

Bob Chandler also had a soft side he rarely displayed in public. He donated money, often quietly out of his own pocket, to various causes. Bob gave college scholarships to nearly 50 young journalists and photojournalists, mostly from Oregon. In later years, he served on the boards of several non-profit agencies. These included the Oregon Community Foundation and The High Desert Museum.

Toward the end of his life, Bob could no longer go into The Bulletin offices. He never lost his love of good writing and his editor's instincts and continued to read at home. One day, while reading a sentimental goodbye article column written by Bob Moody, who was then the publisher of The Observer in La Grande, Chandler looked up and turned to a bystander. "Damn it," he said. "Moody's never going to learn that loan is not a verb."

Excerpted from The Bulletin, July 12, 1996

THE BEND BULLETIN, BEND, OREGON, THURSDAY, JUNE 30, 1932

New Gatekeeper Named By Grange Hall Group

Grange Hall, June 30 – (Special) Louis Roberson has been named gate keeper in Eastern Star grange to succeed C. B. Harvey, who resigned. Harvey is herding his sheep in Bear creek country for the summer.

Speakers at the grange meeting this week were M. A. Lynch, republican candidate for the legislature; Gus Hagglund, county agent; and J. Hilton, representative of the federal land bank. Gene Ackley reported on the state grange convention.

Mrs. Ed Bean was honored with a party by 12 members of the aid society at the home of Mrs. Clarence Smith in Bend last week. Mrs. R. I. Hamby will be hostess for the aid.

CAPITOL—Hurry!

ONLY 2 Days Left

TONIGHT AND FRIDAY

MATINEES AT 2:00

The Horror Picture of the Age

CHILDREN UNDER 12 Not Admitted Unless With Parents

A FRIENDLY WARNING If you have a weak heart and cannot stand intense excitement or even shock, we advise you NOT to see this production. If, on the contrary, you like an unusual thrill, you find it in FRANKENSTEIN

He lives!
He breathes!
He walks!
He sees!
What IS he?
MAN OR MONSTER?

FRANKENSTEIN

THE MAN WHO MADE A MONSTER

The Most Startling Motion Picture Ever Made!

Plan to stay in Bend July 2-3-4
New Picture Each Day st Capitol
Liberty will be opened for three days
WATCH FOR PICTURES

Liberty

FRIDAY NIGHT

Corinne Poindexter's

Dance Revue

One of the most entertaining events of the year. Pupils of all ages ... new costumes ... a credit to any city.

Prices 10c-35c

ENDING WITH TWO SENSAT...

FRIDAY and SA...

MANNHEI...

Announce the Climax Sa...

FINAL WI...

SA...

Final Price Cuts In All...

BUY HERE FOR NATIONAL...

EXTRAORDIN...

Quality Beyond ...

2-Day Sal...

DRESS...

Regular $1....

Dresses 2 f...

Toweling — Bleached or unbleached border. Never so low before. Yard— 5c

Shoes — Over 175 pairs in seven groups. Men's, women's and boys'. Your choice— 1/2 price

Men's Swim Suits — The new speed models in all worsted. Choice patterns. $1.48

Men's Athletic Unions — 29c

Cretonne Pillows — Indispensable for outings and camping. Kapok filled. Each— 28c

GROUP 2

GROUP 3

COAT...

Draperies — 1/2 price

Women's Sweat... $1.2...

Children's Bathing Suits

Corsets Girdles — 1/2 price

Rayon Crepe Slips

...NG WEEK

Now, After a Week of "Comedy"

We settle down to the serious business of cooperating with 10,000 American Legion Posts to aid in a "Business Revival" through this National Buying Week.

Friday and Saturday — SPECIAL — House Frocks — Guaranteed fast color. Regular $1.00 values — Sale 69c

Friday and Saturday — SPECIAL —

Also National Bobolink Week

BOBOLINK HOSIERY Service or chiffon.

The War Years

The things you don't know are
the history you haven't read.

Harry Truman

A Red, White and Blue Job

Loris Farleigh

In 1937, I was appointed Postmaster in Sisters. My beginning salary was a hundred dollars a month, with a fifteen dollar allowance to pay a part-time clerk. I had to augment that out of my own salary. When I took over the Post Office, it was moved to a government owned building that had formerly been the tavern. We furnished and installed the post office boxes, hung the flag and went to work.

I continued in the office until December of 1945. During the time I did that job, we were in the midst of World War II and there were many troops in the area on maneuvers. One morning I went to work and found the Post Office surrounded by cannons. The soldiers had dug foxholes around the area in a mock war. If I'm remembering correctly, they called themselves the Reds and the Blues, and they were all dressed in battle regalia.

Most of the soldiers were from back east, with a lot from big cities like Chicago. Normally Sisters was a small town ... maybe two hundred and fifty patrons, but when you added an army camp with thousands of boys in it, I had my hands full. While they had an APO, or Army Post Office, they just loved to come into our Sisters Post Office to buy money orders to send home. The fact there was no bank in Sisters added to the volume of business we transacted. Mostly they'd just have one-dollar bills, because their chief recreation in camp was playing poker. You are only supposed to have one endorsement on a money order for it to be cashed, but what with all their gambling to pass the time away, they'd sign over some that would have a dozen endorsements on them. Many a night I stayed up until midnight counting one dollar bills, because I had to prepare a transmittal form for every receipt we took in.

One evening, after having closed the Post Office, someone came in and asked if he could buy some stamps. I didn't know who he was, but I was always ready to accommodate anyone, so I sold them to him. He was a very genial man and visited with me for quite some time, asking me about my family and the community and if the boys were bothering me.

At that time I didn't pay much attention to rank. They were all soldier boys to me. While we were talking a buck private came in. He froze at attention when he saw the man who saluted him and said, "At ease." The boy was practically rooted to the spot until after the man walked out. Then he said to me, "M'am, do you know who that man was?" "No," I said, "though I know he is a higher ranking officer." "That," said the young buck private, "was the big guy himself: General George C. Marshall."

From meeting four star generals to counting mountains of dollar bills, running a Post Office surrounded by soldiers in foxholes was an interesting way to help with the war effort without ever leaving home.

As told to Don Ellis
Courtesy of the Redmond Historical Commission

Loris (Henslee) Farleigh, married Dell Louray Farleigh in 1925. They moved to Sisters in 1933 where they owned Farleigh's Service Station until the mid-1940s. After her term as postmistress, Loris worked in a law firm in Redmond for 20 years.

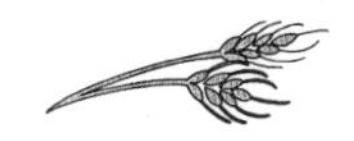

Wartime in Bend

Eva (Dodson) Gassner

I was 16 years old when our neighbor came over and told us about President Roosevelt's address to the nation after Pearl Harbor was bombed. We were at war; we were scared and we were sure we were going to be invaded by the Japanese.

At Bend High School the next day, half the boys - those who weren't already in the National Guard - talked about signing up, and many did, even though they were under age. Their parents vouched for them. Almost as quickly, many young people chose to get married before the war separated them.

Life in Bend and life in general changed. Patriotism became a way of life. Items needed for the war effort like gas, tires, sugar, shortening and shoes were rationed and we learned to make do with what we had, or what we had a coupon for, or we learned to do without. Although we could raise our own food, we couldn't make our own sugar and that caused problems for our regular baking and canning. While rationing was tough, everyone was in the same boat. We conserved everything, including bacon grease which we were told the Government needed for the manufacture of artillery.

The whole population of the town increased because of the military operations in the area. Though the public wasn't allowed anywhere near them, we knew that secret training maneuvers were conducted in the desert near the Redmond Air Base because that area simulated conditions in Africa. Then in November of 1942, construction began on Camp Abbot, the combat engineers' training camp, which was located where Sunriver is now. When it was completed in May of 1943, wives moved to Bend to be nearer their husbands and that created a housing shortage. Many Bend residents rented rooms to them. Restaurants, which had food rationed on the basis of their previous year's use, ran out of food early and closed down at whatever time their daily allotment ran out. Lines at the Liberty and Capitol Theaters ran around the block and it was very hard to see a movie.

Bend residents did all they could to help the war effort in every way they could. Everyone wrote to our men overseas. All through the war I sent letters to our neighbor Bud, who was in the Navy, and my girlfriends all did the same for young men they knew. Ladies, stretching their meager rations, regularly baked their best specialties for the soldiers and hosted in their homes service men in need of a card game, homemade cooking and a feeling of family.

A USO opened in the middle of the block on Wall Street and we local girls were encouraged to go there to entertain the younger soldiers. Mrs. Laura Emard was in charge and she let me in even though I wasn't quite old enough. Two or three times a week I showed up there and she consistently prompted my girlfriends and I - under her watchful, protective eye - to approach shy, isolated men and ask them to dance or to get them involved in playing cards. However, no one was allowed to leave the premises with a man. On the way to the USO we girls stopped by neighbors' houses to collect their cookies and baked goods for the soldiers.

We were dancing fools in those days. We loved ballroom dancing, the jitterbug and the new swing, and if you didn't dance every dance you were considered a wallflower! Dances were the way many people met each other and my girlfriends and I never missed a Saturday dance. I even got to attend some of the dances for officers in the Great Hall at Sunriver. It was common practice in Bend to invite those you met at dances to go to your home for cake and coffee after the last song had played.

Sometime after May 1943, I learned Camp Abbot was hiring women as waitresses, so I applied for a job and I got it. I worked in the gracious hospital dining room which served the doctors, nurses and dentists. About six of the waitresses and other employees on that shift traveled the 14 miles from Bend to Camp Abbot in a green Army bus driven by Mr. McClain. The bus entered under the high wooden gateway labeled "Camp Abbot," which was supported on each end by stanchions resembling castle fortifications. Inside the gates was a world of barracks, mess halls, classroom buildings, warehouses, drill fields, rifle and machine gun ranges, three chapels and combat engineering projects. Marching and walking soldiers and Army vehicles were everywhere.

We worked in the hospital dining room with its white-clothed tables and appealing salads, entrees and desserts, in 12-hour shifts, five days a week. Because we were young, the successive 12-hour shifts were easy for us to work, and I was lucky. Mrs. Bernice Coombs, the corpulent redheaded cook, knew and liked me so I was assigned weekdays for work and had my weekends free. And the money was great! The 25 cents per hour I made was far in excess of the 25 cents I earned for a whole night of baby-sitting or a day of house cleaning.

When school resumed in the fall of 43, I stopped working at Camp Abbot and went back to my studies. The base closed in the summer of 44, having trained tens of thousands of soldiers. While it eventually became just a memory for most people, I retained some relationship to Camp Abbot. I didn't serve any more meals there but after I married Larry Gassner, the son of a cattle rancher, we summered stock on some of that land where so many soldiers had trained a few scant years before.

As told to Karen Goodman

Eva (Dodson) Gassner was born on a ranch in Tumalo in 1925. Her most gratifying work was raising three sons and working with children. Her father, Les Dodson, helped found the Rim Rock Riders Club and Eva is the only living charter member of the club. Her grandfather, Lucius Quintius Cincinnatus, imported the first Black Angus cattle to the Pacific Northwest.

Central Oregon's Fighting 41st

Many young men from Central Oregon served in World War II. One of the outstanding units was the 41st infantry unit, the "Fighting 41st."

The 41st unit was originally formed in 1917 and was the fifth to go to war in France in World War I. The unit was reinitiated in May 1936 when Company I of the Oregon National Guard was formed. At that time, it was an artillery unit with 60 men. Between May 1936 and September 1940, the unit's size fluctuated and it was turned into an infantry unit. Regular drills were held in the Bend Athletic Club gymnasium.

Then in September 1940, Company I was sent to Camp Murray, Washington. It was now 119 infantrymen. Training was intensive but bearable with help from the folks at home.

Pvt. William Stookey, a correspondent for The Bend Bulletin wrote about some of the Unit's experiences at Camp Murray. "Our schedule since arrival in camp has been devoted to preparing comfortable quarters for the winter and gradually bringing the men into condition to withstand the rigorous routine of intensive training. A five-mile hike was taken last week and an eight-mile one this week. These hikes will be made until the men are able to stand twenty-five-miles a day without any effort.

Probably the most comments from other Units in camp about Company I are regarding the large mess fund contributed by the people of Central Oregon. No other Company in camp can claim such backing from Bend, and all Central Oregon. The food is plentiful and well prepared. Our cook's are among the best in camp. Men in other Companies would like to be attached to Company I for meals."

Company I was transformed into the 41st Infantry Unit and on February 28th, 1942 they boarded a train for Ft. Dix, New Jersey. From there they went to New York, boarded ship and sailed through the Panama Canal en route to the South Pacific. The Central Oregonians were among the first to go overseas. They landed in Melbourne, Australia and moved up to Rock Hampton for months of training in jungle combat. They formed the first complete fighting unit in Australia.

The 41st left for combat in New Guinea in April 1944. On July 30th, after 76 continuous days of combat, they drove the Japanese out of the island. Conditions during that campaign were extremely tough.

Dateline: New Guinea ......
...... June 1, 1944 ...... Heavily bearded, longhaired men of Bend's Company I take a much needed rest. "It is plenty hot and the only good water we get is when it rains. A poncho is good for about a fifteen gallon catch." Menu for the day was coffee and crackers for breakfast; Japanese noodles and 'C' rations for dinner; a big batch of rice or if we're lucky, we have some fruit to make rice pudding for supper.

Later, elements of the 41st under General Douglas MacArthur helped to liberate the Philippines and some POWs from Central Oregon.

Dateline: General MacArthur's Headquarters, Leyte Island, Philippines ......October 23, 1944...... Major William C. Chenowith, Bend, Oregon was one of 83 prisoners rescued when a Japanese prison transport was torpedoed by an American submarine. The prisoners were being transported North through the Philippines....Major Chenowith had been a prisoner in the Philippines since the fall of Bataan.

The record of the 41st is impressive. They were the first unit to go overseas, where they served longer than any other unit in the Pacific. They were the first division trained in jungle warfare and fought more campaigns and captured more prisoners (2,200) than any other division. Central Oregon's 'Fighting 41st' was awarded a Presidential Citation and had more individual decorations than any other Army unit in the South Pacific.

Excerpted from The Pioneer Gazette
News excerpts from The Bend Bulletin

Camp Abbot: An Intimate Look at Sunriver's Military History

By Diane M. Roseborough

Before there were luxury homes, a destination resort and miles of paved bike paths, the resort community of Sunriver served as training grounds for the U.S. Army Corps of Engineers during World War II.

It was after the Japanese attack on Pearl Harbor on December 7, 1941, that the Army's Camp Abbot was built on the upper Deschutes River. It was named after retired U.S. Army Brigadier General, Henry Larcom Abbot, a West Point graduate, cited Civil War veteran and Pacific Railroad surveyor. During his time as a group leader in the 1855 Williamson Survey Party that searched for a rail route from the Sacramento Valley to the Columbia River, Abbot traveled through Central Oregon and camped in the broad meadow we now know as Sunriver.

When Camp Abbot opened in early 1943, it spanned nearly 9,700 acres. Commanded by Col. Frank S. Besson, an honors graduate from West Point, the camp trained 90,000 soldiers and other personnel during its 14-month operation.

Most of the high desert areas chosen for training around Camp Abbot were selected for their similarities to European war zones. "We were Col. Besson's troopers," said then Private First Class Don Harrah, who, during his training, came down with pneumonia and nearly lost his life. "We were trained in the winter because we were to go to Europe. We learned how to hide in the snow and get around on skis. We crawled through the infiltration course on our bellies at night with full field packs while they shot machine guns overhead and set off charges around us."

Throughout the camp's operation from March 1943 to June 1944, approximately 10,000 soldiers at a time went through a 17-week three-part training program consisting of general instruction, specialty training and field maneuvers.

Their initial general instruction training lasted six weeks and consisted of map reading, first aid and safeguarding military information. It also included training in hand and anti-tank grenades, and defense against chemical, air and mechanized attack, in addition to rifle marksmanship.

The next segment provided troops with either eight weeks of specialty training in areas of demolition, cooking, administration and automotive operation and maintenance, or technical and tactical training in bridge construction, village fighting and mine field strategy.

The final three week training period was spent in field maneuvers under conditions similar to those of a combat zone. Soldiers would hike 15 to 25 miles to a remote area and simulate battle situations in harsh winter conditions. It was during this last phase when Harrah became deathly ill after being out in the snowy field and spent the next 30 days in the hospital fighting for his life. "It was an interesting winter. I don't know what the winter was, if it was one of the worst or whatever, or if I was just a Southern California boy in the wrong place." Harrah and his group were far from alone in enduring Central Oregon's varying weather conditions as the first trainees who arrived at Camp Abbot in March of 1943 suffered through nighttime temperatures near 20 degrees below zero.

While the extensive and realistic training at the camp turned young men into fighting soldiers, no conditioning could prepare them for all the horrors of war and timing in action. Harrah says as combat engineers, they were usually the first guys in and the last ones to leave. "You send the engineers in first to check out for mines on the bridges, then you remove those and hope you can get some tanks across. If you cannot make it, you get on the other side, but then the panzer division starts shooting at you. Once you back up, the engineers stay behind and either blow up the bridge so they can't get at you or...it's a suicide kind of mission, being an engineer." Harrah knows that well, as the majority of his outfit, the 414th Engineer Group, were killed at the Battle of the Bulge trying to put bridges across the various rivers near Bastogne shortly after leaving Camp Abbot.

Harrah and the other soldiers were trained in building and destroying bridges, but with the exception of the foundation of Besson Bridge, none of the bridges they built remain. The only other remaining structures from Camp Abbot still visible today are the original foundation of the Camp Abbot sign located east of Sunriver's entrance off Highway 97, and the original structure used as the Officers' Club. The Great Hall, as the latter is known today, was constructed by the soldiers with mostly native white fir, ponderosa pine and tamarack. Ten tons of volcanic rock was used to mold the building's fireplaces.

Camp Abbot, like Sunriver today, was a self-contained type of city. It played an important role in our wartime history, both as a training center and as the site of the Oregon Maneuver War games of 1943, the largest maneuver ever held in the Northwest. Those military exercises took place over a 10,000 square mile area in the highlands of Bend, Lakeview, Burns, Prineville, Redmond and Sisters, encompassing much of the area we refer to today as Central Oregon.

Diane M. Roseborough has written for television, radio and newsprint throughout Central Oregon, and has worked in the legal field for over 14 years. Diane moved to Sunriver in 1998 with her husband, Ed and two children, Colin and Nolan.

"Move!" Said the Government

Fannie (Alexander Haberstich) Regnier

At the beginning of World War II the Government condemned some of our property for an airfield, paid us a pittance and told us that we would have to move our house. The Government had us sign a contract pledging the money they would pay for the land and promising a crew to move our house a mile to the north.

That year it rained so hard that the farmers couldn't go into the fields, so my husband Fritz and I sat and watched the equipment being used to build the base get stuck in the mud. Since the fields had been plowed and were soft, the men would no sooner get one rig out than they would have to hook onto another.

The building of the runways was a terrible time for me as the workers picked my garden for a storage area for large machinery and other equipment. After working late of a night, they would begin again at 4:00 a.m., starting motors, running trucks and yelling at each other. When the first runway was blacktopped, it was right by our front door! One evening we could see that a big B-15 was going to land, so we went out into the yard to watch. After it stopped, I discovered that I was on my knees with the shock of witnessing the landing of such a huge airplane right before my eyes.

Weeks went by and no one from the Government showed up to move our house as promised. However, that didn't prevent them from sending orders that if we didn't have the house moved by a certain date they would bulldoze it over and set it on fire. The neighbors helped us get the building off the foundation and onto some huge timbers so it could be pulled to the other side of our property. All this time the rains had continued and the mud was now knee-deep and seemed to have no bottom to it. Once again our thoughtful neighbors came to our assistance and brought in tractors to add to our two. It took a week to pull the house a mile with five big tractors. When the move was done it was in shambles with part of the floor torn out. You couldn't buy lumber as the Government used every bit of it and there wasn't a vacant house for 50 miles. So we had no choice but to live in it just the way it was. It was a cold winter and we had to wear heavy clothes in the house all the time until the bedroom floors were repaired after the war was over.

Ironically, the airbase that deprived us of our home provided a civil service job for me. Workers were desperately needed, so I signed up to be a chauffeur. Except for our five-year-old, our kids were in school. Our only option was for him to stay with his dad while he worked the fields. After several months serving as a chauffeur, Major Arnold, the Base Commander, selected me to be his driver. Although there were a thousand men there at times, I was soon elevated to take over the motor pool office for all the base vehicles. I didn't think I could do it but the commander said he knew I could.

In addition to driving, I was appointed to be base hostess for their parties. Whichever group was to have a party told me and would send a vehicle to get me and take me home when it was over. Several of the men wanted a date, but I always told them I was a happy, married woman. I guess that, plus the fact I never drank or smoked, is why I was selected to help with those social activities.

There was one awful incident, however. There were two little buildings off to one side by themselves. One was for the high-ranking officer who was in command of all the buildings. Two girls worked in one building and one in the other. One day, after they had all arrived at work, the high-ranking officer brought in a can of gas, set it by the stove, walked out and it exploded. While one girl escaped from a window and was badly burned, the others did not get out. When they investigated, they discovered the big Muck was one of those working for Hitler - right there in our midst!

When the war was over I received a pin from the Government for my good conduct, but we never got our land back. The City of Redmond got it for an airport instead.

As told to Karen Goodman

Fannie Alexander Regnier was born in 1905 near Culver. She has lived in Central Oregon all her life. She and her late husband farmed until 1965. She has 4 children; 3 live in Central Oregon.

Some Fought While Others Were Asked To Farm

Sid Elliott

I was born in Terrebonne on my father's homestead in 1914. Later, in 1920, we relocated from the north to 160 acres on the south side of Cinder Hill. Economically that turned out to be a good move, but it sure involved a lot of hard work. Initially there were only four acres cleared. Until Dad built a house for us we lived in a shack that had a little lean-to on the back of it and he fixed a tent for us boys to sleep in.

The year I was a freshman in high school we had a party at the house and Mrs. Hirsch, our algebra teacher, told my folks, "You'd better be getting that boy to college." That just put a thought in my mind and I decided I was gonna go even though there was no way my parents could afford to send me. About 2 years later, when my sister Maxine graduated as the valedictorian of her class, a fellow from Pacific University came over to offer her a scholarship. However, she wasn't ready to go, so my dad said, "Why don't you talk to Sid?" That's how I got a scholarship to Pacific University.

While it paid my tuition, I was still responsible for my room and board. I had saved up 65 dollars but that wasn't enough to cover it so I had to find a place where I could work. First I went to see the registrar and asked if he could find work for me. "In the meantime," he asked, "do you have any place to stay?" When I said no, he suggested I go over to McCormick Hall where the football players were practicing and eat with them. Then he added, "You might have to practice with 'em." I did that for three days and I found out I could run with them, but I didn't bump with 'em too good.

The year I was a junior, Jack Whiteside asked me if I would like to work as the backroom boy at his hardware store. That was a great experience because he kept calling me over to where he was working and showing me what he was doing. I think I learned more in that back room about how a business was run than I learned from any class I took. In 1940 I graduated as an honor student with a major in Animal Science, but I returned home and eventually ended up being a crop farmer.

I was on a horse on Sunday afternoon, December 7, 1941 knocking a ball around with a polo mallet when I stopped for a minute to go to the house and found out Pearl Harbor had been attacked. My involvement in the war effort was as a farmer because I was chosen to stay home and produce. That meant I had to work awfully hard. One of the things I did in the wintertime to make a contribution was to help other farmers sort their potatoes. I raised potatoes until problems with my shoulder forced me to move on to something else.

After the war I was one of the first peppermint growers in Jefferson County. I had 20 or so acres to start with. Later I got started in grass seed and I think that was my favorite crop. It was certainly good for the soil because blue grass puts down lots of roots and you don't have any erosion.

It was good to go away to school and it was good to come home and work the land. Many of the young men from Central Oregon were drafted or enlisted and fought the war on far off shores, but I was asked to stay behind and farm. I did my part right here at home, planting and harvesting food to feed those hungry troops.

As told to Cynthia Larkin
Courtesy of the Redmond Historical Commission

Sid Elliott, was born in Terrebonne in 1914. After college he began farming in partnership with his father. He retired from active farming in 1992. He lives in Redmond and assists his daughter Leslie as she farms the family land.

Jack Brinson

Jack Brinson joined the National Guard at age 15 because he wanted to play basketball. When the captain asked his age he said "15." "No," said the captain pointing to the registration paper: "How old are you?" "Eighteen," Jack replied, and he was sworn in. On September 16, 1940, the National Guard was mobilized into Federal service because the government knew it looked like war. Jack left the family homestead in northeast Bend where Brinson Boulevard is now, and was with his Army unit at Hickam Field in Hawaii, waiting to be shipped out to the Philippines on December 7, 1941, the day the Japanese bombed Pearl Harbor.

Jack Brinson, was born in 1920 on a ranch that his parents homesteaded near Bend. He had a 35 year career with the telephone company. He received the Silver Star and four Purple Hearts for his exceptional service in the war.

We Danced Away The Years

Jessie Taylor

When WW II was over, the young people coming back from the service needed a place to get acquainted and reacquainted and to get to know the people and the town. After a branch of the nationwide Junior Chamber of Commerce was started in Redmond, some of the wives got together and decided to be Jaycettes to fill that gap. Those were pre-TV days and we had to have something to do for entertainment, to mingle, have fun and forget our troubles.

We met first at Fran Munkres house, elected officers, then met monthly in member's homes. For entertainment we sponsored two or three dances a year, a New Years Dance, a spring dance and sometimes one in the fall. We would have an orchestra come in from Bend to play good dance music and added a little floorshow whenever we could. These public dances were held in Townsend Hall, which I think is now the Elks, the Redmond Grange and the Pleasant Ridge Grange.

Dancing was so popular that some of us also organized a dance club, which we called the 70 and Five because we limited it to 75 couples. We met at the old Officers' Club at the airbase every winter month except December. Once a year we had a costume dance and one time a fellow came holding an iron gate in front of him and said he was the Iron Curtain in Russia. For about 20 years we danced our way through life with that group, but it finally disbanded when it became too hard to find an orchestra to play good dance music.

As told to Lorna Cerenzia

Jessie M. Taylor, was born in Prosser, Washington in 1920. She moved to Redmond in 1944. She has been an active volunteer in addition to raising her family.

And Then There Was Mt. Bachelor

Success is peace of mind
and a feeling of
well -being within yourself.

Nick Reynolds,
Co-Founder of the Kingston Trio

Bill, The Boss

Kathy DeGree

One day in November 1973, Bill Healy walked up to me and said, "I see you sitting around the lodge from time to time. Do you want to work?" I wasn't really looking for a job, but he kept after me. Then one day he asked again. I was resting in the lodge after a day of skiing and I said, "O.K.," never dreaming how long my Bachelor adventure would last.

It was a fun winter. Initially I worked in the rental shop but I really found my niche the next year when Bill asked me to work with him on public relations. Bill was really a great mentor. He gave me opportunities to become a member of the management team and was always there to support my efforts.

The lift lines needed to change. He wanted to make waiting fun, so Bill came up with the idea of lift hostesses which he called 'Bachelor Girls', the official ticket checkers. The 'Bachelor Girls' became the guest relation greeters and worked at keeping everybody happy.

Bill wanted to develop a marketing and strategic business plan to present to the Board of Directors, and gave me the opportunity to work with him on it. Bill asked me to present a plan and that continued my career on the management track.

Although Bill was the boss, I don't think I ever heard those words come out of him. He brought out the best in everybody. It was never about himself. It was always about whomever he was with. It was about we and you, not about I. Bill was creative and a problem solver who had the ability to take the bad and turn it into good. He always saw the opportunities, not the barriers.

During the snow drought of 1976, which was long before the slopes were groomed, it took a lot of white stuff on the ground to keep Bachelor open. Many of the Northwest ski areas shut down but Bill knew there would be a way for the mountain to open. At that time he owned Healy's Furniture and one day he brought yards and yards of carpet remnants up to the mountain and the employees rolled the carpet out on the slopes. The employees wore backpacks with water in them and we sprayed the carpets so they'd ice up for skiing. He then designed a machine to spray water on the slopes to do a better job of icing. That meant that the ski area was open and people had jobs. To Bill it wasn't so much about opening the ski area; it was making sure that everyone had a job. He understood the economic windfall and the value of Mt. Bachelor to the community.

Then came the rains in January. All the snow washed down the slope and as a result, a big lake formed in front of the lodge. There weren't very many of us up there, about a 100 or so, and he pulled us all together and said, "I hate to tell you guys, but we're gonna have to lay you all off." Then the very next day he called every one of us to say that he had found us a job. He knew and we knew because Bend was so small, there wasn't going to be work for many of us in town. Bill valued his employees and went out of his way to take care of them the best he could.

Then came the oil embargo with the long gas lines creating some interesting circumstance for Mt. Bachelor too. No gas and no fuel meant no diesel to run the lifts. Once again Bill's ingenuity brought a solution. Bill put together a group and I don't know how he did it, but we had fuel. He bought a gas station and everyone went there at night and filled up when the lights were out. You never knew when you'd get the ticket to go. Bill figured this was a way for our out-of-town guests to get gas to travel back home. Everyone took turns working there, so when our guests left the mountain, they came in and they got just enough gas to get them home.

Bill Healy was one of our community's great leaders. He knew that the mountain needed the community and the community needed Mt. Bachelor. With him, it was always about togetherness.

As told to Richard Gorman

Kathy DeGree, b. 1950 in Auburn, California. She came to Bend in 1973 with a degree from Fresno State University in speech pathology. She worked at Mt. Bachelor from 1973 until 2001.

Chris Hart

My dad, Bill Healy, moved our family to Bend from Portland sometime in 1950. My grandfather owned furniture manufacturing businesses and furniture stores in Bend, Redmond, Prineville and The Dalles. Although Dad had a degree in forestry, he moved to Central Oregon to take over the stores.

Initially, Dad went back and forth between Mt. Bachelor and the stores. In the winter he was at the furniture store during the week and on Sundays he was at the mountain. Ultimately he sold the stores but he was involved with Mt. Bachelor right up until the time he died.

As told to Richard Gorman

Chris Hart was born in Portland in 1949. She came to Bend in 1950 where she attended school and then University of Oregon. She was a flight attendant for United Airlines and is now owner of the Old Mill Market and Deli.

Volunteers Build A Mountain

Don & Ollie Peters

It was 1943 when Don and Ollie Peters first started going through Bend. Don had an appointment with the Forest Service in Lakeview, Ollie's folks were up in the Mount Hood Forest, and they frequently traveled the road in between. They did a lot of shopping in Bend and liked what they saw here. Their boys did too, and whenever they were in town they always said, "We have to go to the Pine Tavern."

When the Forest Service transferred Don to Bend in 1956, they provided the area with a key person for the development of Mt. Bachelor, for he had been instrumental in developing the Warner Canyon Ski Area in Lakeview and was on the National Ski Patrol too. Both positions ultimately proved to be valuable assets. In the meantime, he was put in charge of all the fire control activities and, in addition, monitored Forest Service permits for summer homes and recreational uses of the land.

"I got acquainted with Bill Healy when we first came to town," Don said. "He had a furniture store and Ollie was down there a lot." "Well, we needed some furniture," she said, "and Bill was a very friendly type." It wasn't long before Bill and Don were discussing skiing and the fact the only ski hill in the area was Skyliners. When Don suggested to Bill that they find another place to ski, the site he proposed was Bachelor Butte, but Bill said the Forest Service wouldn't allow the development of a ski resort there. His comments were a challenge to Don, who was in charge of administering all the leases and doing all the government work for special use permits. And so their work began.

First they were required to throw the ski area development idea open to competition. "It was necessary for the Forest Service to contact all Washington, Oregon, California, Rocky Mountain and Northeastern major ski area operators to determine if there were other likely prospects for the proposed development at Mt. Bachelor," Don said, "but no one was interested. They said, 'You haven't got enough population in Bend. People that ski out of Portland go to Mt. Hood, and people from Corvallis that ski go to Hoodoo'." That attitude didn't deter Healy or the Peters. "We knew people would make the drive to Central Oregon for fine powder," said Ollie.

Although competition was a non-issue, they still needed construction funds and a volunteer ski patrol to establish a new ski area. During the summer of 56 they worked on getting stockholders. "I would go out and give speeches at the various civic clubs," Don said, "and Healy canvassed the motels. There were about thirty of them in town. They'd operate during the summer and then when hunting season was over they folded up. There were only one or two of them that stayed open during the winter." Despite the promise of potential customers, he said, "there wasn't one of the owners of the motels that wanted to buy any stocks." Because of his position with the Forest Service, Don could not buy stock himself as it would be a conflict of interest.

He could work on the development as a volunteer though, and he put thousands of unpaid hours into the project. As Ollie indicated, they had both always been very active in their community and "when we moved here it was just a continuation of our volunteering."

Don had quite a lot of experience in skiing and in first aid and he was the only person east of the Cascades who was certified to train other people to become Red Cross First Aid Instructors. The next extension of that activity was organizing and training the ski patrol for Mount Bachelor. Don recruited volunteers and trained them in first aid, avalanche control and other essential skills.

"Eventually, we had about twenty or thirty volunteers on the ski patrol," Don added, "including several doctors. You had to be a real good skier, and you had to be pretty strong to use the equipment." Like Don, the patrol members all worked during the week and spent their weekends on the mountain volunteering their services. "I don't think we'd have Mt.

Bachelor today if it hadn't been for those volunteers," he concluded.

Don was also instrumental in initiating search and rescue operations at Mt. Bachelor. Perhaps he did it in self-defense so he wouldn't have to rescue everyone himself. As he recalled, the road wasn't wide open to Bachelor like it is now. Sometimes in the wintertime at the lower elevation there would be quite a bit of snow. A number of people who headed for the mountain thought they were hardy pioneers. Some of them were, but some of them got lost. When that happened, they'd call the state police. And the state police would say that's not our responsibility, call the sheriff. And then they'd call the sheriff and the sheriff would say that if it was an emergency the state police were responsible. Since they didn't have anybody trained to do search and rescue, they called Don and he often wound up going out by himself on cross-country skis to get them.

Nor is that all he did, for Don was also responsible for safety inspections at Mt. Bachelor, and in that capacity he designed an electrical circuit, which was an adaptation of one he had seen at another resort. When a skier went past a certain point on a rope tow it broke that circuit and stopped the tow, which in turn prevented the serious accidents and occasional deaths that happened elsewhere when clothing or long hair froze to the tow rope.

When talking about the mountain, Don is quick to credit the volunteers who gave so much of themselves to establish the ski resort on Mt. Bachelor. "Makes you really appreciate people who volunteer, doesn't it," he said. And when credit is given where credit is due, Don Peters will be remembered as the man who volunteered to build a mountain.

As told to Ray Miao

Don b. Twin Falls, ID 1912 and Ollie b. White Bear Lake, MN 1919. Don and Ollie married in 1937. They moved to Lakeview in 1943 and Bend in 1956. Don worked for the Forest Service in range and watershed surveys, and was fire boss on large fires. Ollie worked for Wetle's Dept. Store and Ray LeBlanc's Men's Store. They have 2 sons.

CAT On The Summit

Ron Robinson Sr.

Three generations of our family work together here in Central Oregon. It all began when my dad moved to the area in 1947.

Without stretching things a bit, you could say that we did the highest work in Central Oregon. Not price-wise. I'm talking about elevation, for we worked on the last lift on Mr. Bachelor that went to the summit.

There was a bet....I bet 'em I could put a CAT on top of Mt. Bachelor. They said I couldn't. I said, O.K., if I can put the CAT on top of Mt. Bachelor, we're gonna work up there and it's gonna be x amount of dollars, and they said O.K. I said if I can't put it up there you don't have to pay anything. Well, we did it and we got paid.

I spent a couple days walking the area and we mapped out a trail of where we planned to put the CAT. However, after about the first half-mile, we went a different way and took the CAT right across the snow-fields.

I got the job, and it was a tremendous amount of work, probably the most challenging job we ever had. You're in a different world up there. When you get icicles hangin' on your eyebrows and your nose, you know it's cold.

There's a lot more room up there. More than you think. It isn't a point. It's an interesting summit and we put a CAT up there when no one thought we could.

As told to Charlene & David Blahnik

Ron Robinson's father Jack started Robinson & Sons Construction. It is the oldest family-owned business of its size in Oregon.

Skiing Pioneers

Jane Meissner Ford

We started skiing really young. All three of the kids in our family, my sister Julie and my brother Ernie, I'm the middle one; we started skiing when we were about a year and a half. I was nineteen months old when I was on skis. I don't remember learning how to ski, it was just something we always did.

My mom, Virginia Meissner, went to college at U. of O. and became friends with the outdoor people there. She learned how to ski at Willamette Pass, which is up by Odell Lake. She met my dad, Jack, there. He was teaching skiing on weekends there at Willamette. They got married in 1949.

My dad and his mom owned the marina up at the west end of Odell Lake. My mom and dad's house was closer to the highway. It was real hard to make a living up there in the winter. So my mom and my dad both taught skiing on the weekends. During the week my dad had trap lines. My dad would bring the animals home then Mom got the job of taking the skins off and stretching and tanning them. She also would help us kids set out little trap lines. We had three traps and she helped us ski around to the different traps. I remember getting a mink one time. Dad would go off for four or five days at a time and he'd trap a lot of bears. He'd sell the bear fur and we'd eat a lot of bear meat.

One winter while on a 200 mile cross country ski trip from Mt. Hood to Crater Lake my dad tested clothing for the While Stag company. He wore pants that had one leg made out of wool and the other out of their synthetic fabric. Two friends started the trip with him but dropped out after two weeks. He spent a lot of time breaking trail, and for a couple days he was stuck in a storm in a little, tiny tent, afraid he would run out of food. When the weather cleared he was able to finish that incredible trip alone in the midst of winter.

The year that Mt. Bachelor opened, 1958, we started driving over to Bend so that Mom and Dad could teach down hill skiing. We drove every weekend for two years before we moved to Bend for the winters and stayed at Odell Lake in the summers.

A couple of years after my parents started teaching at Bachelor my Dad became the Assistant Ski School Director, and then, after a couple more years, Director. Together they ran the school as a franchise operation and, in addition, coached the Mitey Mites.

They bought ten acres out on Denser Road which is now 27th Street. It was a double A frame house, three stories tall. I'd never seen a house like it and I haven't seen one since. We hauled water from a place down by Pioneer Park. You could fill up your tank for a quarter. First we hauled it in the back of an old pickup. Then we had a pump to pump it upstairs to the third floor to a tank. It would gravity feed to the floors down below. When we'd think that maybe we were getting out of water then we'd run upstairs and move the top off the tank and look and see how much water we had left. They took the house down right shortly after my mom died. There's about thirty houses on our ten acres now.

It was in probably the early sixties that the college was interested in offering cross-country ski classes. My dad was on the US Cross Country Ski Team for a couple of years. So my mom and my dad started teaching students. Sometimes Mom and her students would get off trail. They'd be going cross country and they'd be going up and down hills and through the bushes and across streams. The students worried 'how are we going to get back down from here'. She knew that she could get them down safely but they'd all have this little bit of worry in their mind. She was the first recipient of the Outstanding Instructor of the Year Award from COCC's Community Education Division in 1987.

The classes interested people in skiing and sparked other people to try a little bit more cross country. So she just got friends that wanted to ski and in conjunction with the Forest Service, started laying out a few trails. Then they started the Central Oregon Chapter of the Oregon Nordic Club. Once they did that, they worked with the Forest Service to lay out all the trails and the shelter placements. She was in on helping lay those out, and helped to build them all.

There's a snow park named after her. She had already been skiing in that area on old Forest Service roads. So she approached the Forest Service about making some of those Forest Service roads marked cross country ski trails. The Forest Service had a whole process to consider what other options the area could be used for. The options were that it could be a cross country skiing area, a snow mobile area, or it could be a combined use area. She spearheaded working with the Nordic Club and land owners in the Tumalo Creek area who submitted a petition. That was the final convincing thing to the Forest Service and it was designated just for cross country skiing. My mom was always rather humble but after her death they named it the Virginia Meissner Snow Park.

They both taught skiing at Mt. Bachelor for about 20 years. After trying to retire, Jack returned to Willamette Pass Ski Area and was ski school director there for over 15 years. He still lives out in the Odell Lake area. At 82 he still skis and does the cabin and dock maintenance and repair work he has been doing every summer since 1947.

As told to Carol Swift

The Mitey Mites

Rosanna (Burgess) Duberow

I may not have had skis before I could walk, but I don't remember a time before I was strapping them on my feet. I grew up in a lumber camp and used old skis and cross-countried with them. We slid down the hills and used stumps to build jumps. My husband Barney started skiing as a kid in Erie, PA on old pine boards. He picked up alpine skiing when he was transferred to the Sisters Ranger District the year before we were married.

We had four kids and they learned to ski at Hoodoo and Mt. Hood. Then Barney was transferred from the Ochoco Ranger Station to Bend in 1957, the year before Bachelor opened.

Initially the new Bachelor ski resort had only rope tows and a Poma lift. The Poma is a disk on a pole attached to the lift. You put the disk between your legs, hang onto the pole, and it pulls you up the hill. It was one step up from a rope tow and a giant step down from the chairs that ultimately replaced both the rope tows and the Poma. Skiing was different in those days. The clothes weren't as warm, the equipment wasn't as sophisticated and you had to learn how to ski powder because the slopes weren't groomed. But none of that kept it from being a lot of fun.

Not too long after Bachelor opened, Jack and Virginia Meissner began bringing their children, Julie, Jane and Ernie over from the Willamette Pass. At first they brought their trailer house and parked it in our driveway for the weekend. It was a cooperative arrangement that worked well and we enjoyed having many suppers together.

Barney and I volunteered to teach beginners in the Skyliner Ski School. I stayed on and taught in the Mt. Bachelor Ski School for Joe Ward and then for Jack Meissner after Joe retired. Jack Meissner started the Mitey Mite racing program for children 12 and under.

Originally there were about 35 or 40 Mitey Mites including our four kids, Gerry, Fred, Marianne and Robin. All of the kids were on skis by the time they were 5 or 6. I remember, in early December the kids in the program went up to the mountain on two Saturdays for free or very inexpensive lessons and skiing. A lot of people helped out with the program and the kids learned a lot by following the good skiers around.

There were different age classes with separate races for the boys and girls, but sometimes they had co-ed races too. Mt. Bachelor helped with the cost of running the races and was very cooperative throughout the years, preparing the slopes while the parents, who did most of the volunteer work, watched the gates and kept the times. Eventually the Mitey Mite program was taken over first by the Skyliner Ski Club and then by the Mt. Bachelor Ski Education Foundation.

I think the years Barney and I spent transporting carloads of kids to races on other mountains, the hundreds of sack lunches I packed, the wet clothes we crammed in full cars, paid off in more ways than one. It was a wonderful opportunity for our family to work and play together, and three of our four kids went to college on full or partial ski scholarships.

Now all our kids are grown and we're retired. But skiing is still a part of our lives. We watch for the first snowflakes to fall and we spend one or two days a week on the slopes throughout the season. We definitely appreciate the smooth grooming these days. But we don't ski when we can't see. At least not more than a run or two.

As told to Richard Gorman

Rosanna (Burgess) Duberow was born in Bend in 1923 and was raised in the Shevlin-Hixon logging camps in the La Pine area. After college at Oregon State University she married Barney Duberow. In addition to raising four children she taught in the Bend schools.

It is when we forget outselves
that we do things
that are likely to be remembered.

Unknown